PROPERTY
INVESTMENT
FOR
BEGINNERS

PROPERTY INVESTMENT FOR BEGINNERS:

A Property Geek Guide

Rob Dix

CONTENTS

LEARN WHAT'S WORKING IN PROPERTY RIGHT NOW

This book is designed to give you a fun, accessible overview of property investment. There's always plenty more to learn, though – especially as the market is changing all the time.

To deepen your knowledge and keep up with all the changes, there are two things you should do.

First, sign up for my weekly newsletter at **property-geek.net/newsletter**. Every Sunday I share the top property stories of the week with a short explanation of why they matter.

Then, visit **propertyhub.net** (which I co-founded) where we publish free courses, videos, a weekly podcast, and more – and you can join the Property Hub community to benefit from the knowledge of thousands of other investors.

I'll see you there!

A PEP TALK FOR 2021

Every December, I update this book to make sure it accurately reflects the state of the market and includes the latest legal and tax changes. After I've read it through and laughed at my own jokes for the millionth time, it's always interesting to reflect on how much has changed in such a short space of time.

When I wrote the first edition of this book in 2013, all the talk was of "negative growth" (one of my favourite euphemisms) in the economy, and whether the UK would lose its AAA credit rating. House prices had just started to show their first increases since the meltdown of 2008, but memories of the chaos were still fresh – and if you walked through an estate agent's door with an intention to buy, you'd be greeted like a minor celebrity.

Fast forward a few years, and it was like the whole crisis never happened. Low interest rates and more relaxed attitudes to lending saw mortgage applications rocket, the "house prices soar to new heights" headlines came back, and estate agents recovered much of their characteristic smugness.

Normally, the government of the day would look approvingly at these events. When house prices are going up it makes existing homeowners happier – and more inclined to vote for the same colour next time. This time, though, things are different. Since 2015 politicians have been pulling out all the stops to discourage the whole enterprise of buy-to-let, amid concerns that investors are out-bidding owner-occupiers for the limited supply of available housing and contributing to ever-increasing inequality.

The political rights and wrongs of the situation could be debated for hours, but the end result is that your ambition isn't going to earn you any high-fives from our friends in Westminster. Over the last few years we've seen major tax and legislative changes designed to trip up existing investors and discourage new ones (discussed in full later), and it wouldn't surprise me if there were more to come.

And then 2020 happened. The measures taken to contain Covid affected everyone and everything – and as I write this in January 2021, the potential for further economic fallout is making many people even less inclined to invest.

Strange as it may seem, I believe this is a good thing.

Why? Because the more people who sell up or are deterred from entering the market, the better it is for the rest of us. Fewer buyers scrambling for properties means we can buy them cheaper. Fewer available rental properties means higher rents, and the ability to be more selective about the tenants we choose.

Yes, investing in residential property involves more effort and knowledge than it did before. This is bad news if you just wanted to pick up an extra house to gloat about at dinner parties, but doesn't stop property from being the unbeatable vehicle for accumulating long-term wealth that it's been for hundreds of years. It's also, importantly, good news for tenants – who deserve to have a landlord who takes their responsibilities seriously.

So use the principles in this book to make fully informed, long-term investments that put more money in your pocket than costs and taxes take out. Whenever you see a headline about how the buy-to-let era is over, be delighted – because it's just deterred another batch of potential competitors. And when you look at the value of your investments in 20 years' time, prepare to be very, *very* glad that you took the plunge.

ABOUT ME

My name's Rob, and I'm an obsessive researcher.

I can't buy an electric shaver without having 20 browser tabs open. If I discover a new band I like, by the end of the afternoon I'll know the life story of the members and exactly what other music influenced them. And let's not even get started on booking flights.

Unusually, all this went out of the window when I bought my first flat: I just wanted a home that was both affordable and convenient to get back to after late-night DJing gigs.

So I found two ex-council flats ten minutes from King's Cross station, briefly viewed them both, and bought one. Job done. I wasn't remotely fazed by the bulletproof glass at the counter of the local McDonalds, or the exotic array of substances and services being offered on street corners – and I'm not sure I even bothered to negotiate the asking price. (By pure luck, the area has undergone massive regeneration and it's now easier to buy a kale smoothie than anything illicit.)

Then a couple of years later – when I had some spare cash saved up and was considering investing it in another property – I reverted to type. I spent hours and hours browsing internet message boards, reading up on different strategies, and phoning people for advice. Before I knew it I had colour-coded spreadsheets, piles of scribbled notes, and lengthy email chains with people who were kind enough to feed my new addiction.

While doing all this research, I was surprised by the lack of resources for beginners: there was barely anything that gave them an overview of property investment as a whole. As a dedicated researcher I enjoyed digging through forums for pearls of wisdom, but it was a bit like trying to learn French by reading Le Monde every day: you'll get there in the end, but it'd be a damn sight quicker if you learnt some basic vocabulary and grammar first.

The only books I could find were by people who'd found great success with one particular strategy and then written a book about how they did it. That's great, but who's to say that the same approach would mesh with my skills, goals and personality?

So, seven years on from that first flat, while travelling the world with my wife funded partially by the rental profits of the properties we've accumulated since, I started blogging about property at **propertygeek.net**. As a result of that blog, I've gone on to write four books, co-found a company that both provides a vast amount of free education *and* sources and manages properties (**propertyhub.net**), and present the UK's most popular business podcast (**propertyhub.net/ podcast**).

In short, I'm only a small-scale investor. I can't tell you the formula for how I made countless millions, because I haven't. I can't walk you step-by-step through a large-scale development project, because I haven't done that either. I absolutely can't tell you how to do a full refurb on your own, because the last time I tried to fit a self-closing fire door it took me a week.

That's fine: there are experts in all those areas who can tell you those things. What I *can* do is give you the benefit of my research – both from reading and the connections I've built – to give you a relatively bias-free overview of the options available to you. I can also lecture you on the mindset and skills you need to develop a property business that can give you life-changing freedom… because I *have* done that.

My aim is to present all this stuff in a way that's clear, honest, and fun to read. I hope you enjoy it, and more importantly, I hope you do something with it.

Rob Dix

January 2021

INTRODUCTION

How many of your family and friends have talked about getting involved in property investment? I'm going to guess it's quite a lot.

People think of property as an exciting investment option – even when they'd never dream of investing in shares, bonds or other types of asset. Why is this?

I think it comes down to three main reasons:

1.   **Property is tangible**. You can see it, work on it, have opinions on it, and show it off to your friends. And everyone needs to live in one, whether they own it or not.

2.   **Property offers unusually high potential returns because of leverage**. In other words, banks will lend you the majority of the money you need to invest, which amplifies your own

potential gains. That's pretty unique: a bank wouldn't lend you money so you could dabble in buying classic cars, or gold. (If you don't understand leverage fully, don't worry – that's the subject of the first chapter.)

3.   **Property has some kind of intrinsic value.** You could argue all day about what a particular property is "worth", but it's clear that it's worth something – if you buy a house, there will be some non-zero price that you can either rent it out for or sell it for. That's not at all like shares or precious metals, where your investment can tumble by 90% because there's been a shift in the general consensus of opinions that sets a selling price.

So that's why I think property is popular. The reason it's so exciting to me is that you can approach it in so many different ways. If you're a hands-on, DIY-blessed person, you can make great profits by buying an unloved property and restoring it to former glories. Or if you don't know one end of a hammer from the other, you can outsource that part and concentrate on negotiating brilliant deals from people who are in a bind and need to sell quickly. Or even if you've got no special skills at all, you can still make good returns by buying sensibly, understanding the numbers, and holding on for the long term.

But if you think back to all your family and friends who've talked about dabbling in property, you'll have probably found that most of them haven't done anything about it. That's understandable: buying property involves large sums of money, and it's a scary thing. It's easy to feel like you don't have the knowledge or the skills to make a go of it. However vivid your property dreams, pulling the trigger by slapping down thousands of pounds and acquiring a debt of many thousands more isn't easy to do.

The aim of this book is to give you the knowledge and perspective you need to make your first steps in property investment – or start doing it more seriously if you've just been dabbling and want to take it further.

I don't want to persuade you to go about things in a certain way, nor do I promise to tell you everything there is to know about each strategy. Instead, I hope to give you a grip of the fundamentals of what property investment is all about (in Part 1), take you through some of the common approaches and techniques people use (in Part 2), and finally (in Part 3) go more into the mindset you'll need to adopt to be a successful property investor.

After that, it's up to you. Hopefully you'll have a fresh outlook on what property investing is all about, and you'll find yourself particularly intrigued by at least a couple of the strategies we discuss. Then it's time to read further and deeper about the aspects that interest you – I list plenty of resources for further reading at the end – and get started. After all, you'll only learn so much from reading around the subject – the best learning comes from experience.

So, let's get started. Before we jump into the topic of leverage and why it's such a wonderful thing, we just need to take a look at the world's shortest glossary.

THE WORLD'S SHORTEST GLOSSARY

This book doesn't contain many specialist or technical terms, and most of them get explained along the way.

But there are just two terms that are so fundamental to the whole shebang that it's worth making sure we're totally clear on them right from the start. Here's your incentive for learning them: they're both related to someone giving you money, which you can use to go out and buy property.

Loan-to-value (LTV)

The acronym "LTV" crops up a lot when it comes to mortgages. It's one of those things that's only self-explanatory when you already know what it means:

it's the loan (amount you're borrowing) as a propor-tion of the value (of the thing you're buying).

LTV is always expressed as a percentage, such as 75%. A LTV of 75% just means that you've been loaned 75% of the value. In other words, if you put in the cash for 25% of the house you're buying, the lender will give you the other 75%.

Before the last recession happened and everyone real-ised that things like this were a terrible idea, it was possible to get a LTV of 110%. Yep, that means they'd lend you all the money you needed to buy the house, plus 10% more.

We'll discover in Chapter 1 why this is such a spectac-ularly bad move.

Equity

Equity is best thought of as the amount you'd have left over if you sold a property and paid off any loans secured against it. It can be expressed as a percentage, or an amount in itself.

If you bought a property worth £100,000 using all your own cash, your equity would clearly be £100,000. But let's say you bought a house worth £100,000 by getting a loan for three-quarters of that amount (a 75% LTV, right?) and putting in the other quarter yourself. That means you'd have equity of 25%, or £25,000. Same thing.

If the value of that house doubled to £200,000, your loan would have remained the same so your equity would now be £125,000, or 62.5%.

PART 1:
BASIC INVESTMENT PRINCIPLES

Chapter 1
Leverage

Leverage is a word that people in property throw around a lot, and you probably have a rough sense of what it means: boosting your returns, or something like that.

But leverage is something that becomes more awesome the more you think about it, and explains why property is such a great thing to invest in.

Like the name suggests, leverage acts like a lever: by applying a small force at one end, you can produce a bigger force at the other. And the longer the lever, the bigger the amplification effect.

In the case of property investment, the small force you put in is your deposit, and the lever is a mortgage.

A quick mortgage primer

In subsequent chapters we'll discuss mortgages in more detail, but for now we just have to understand one thing: how to calculate what the monthly cost of the mortgage will be.

If a mortgage has an interest rate of 5%, it means that every year you'll have to pay the lender 5% of the total amount you borrowed. So if you borrow £100,000, the annual interest will be £5,000.

To work out how much that would cost each month, you just divide £5,000 by 12, to arrive at £416.6666667 (recurring. Does anyone else wish they'd decimalise the calendar to make the maths easier?).

It's important to realise that at the end of the year when you've paid your £5,000 in interest, you still owe the original £100,000. That's because we're talking about interest-only mortgages – the most common type used in property investment. We'll talk about the difference between interest-only and capital repayment mortgages later on.

Using a mortgage to amplify your return on investment

Here's a not-at-all-made-up example of how using a mortgage can amplify your return on investment:

Deep-pockets Dave has a spare £100,000 burning a hole in his Coutts account. He uses it to buy a house outright – no mortgage. Ten years later, the house is worth £200,000, and he sells it. That's a 100% return on investment. Not too shabby!

Mortgage-lover Mandy has £25,000 in her savings account, and takes out a mortgage for £75,000 so that she too can buy a house worth £100,000. Her house is also worth £200,000 in ten years, so once she's paid back the mortgage she's left with £125,000. That's a 400% return on investment!

Leveraged Leon only has £10,000, but talks his bank into lending him the £90,000 he needs to buy the £100,000 house. By the time it's spookily gone up in value by exactly the same amount as Dave and Mandy's houses, he's left with £110,000 in his pocket after paying back the mortgage – a 1,000% return on his investment!

Leverage don't come for free

Banks don't lend money for nowt, so there'll be interest to pay on that leverage.

But say it's a buy-to-let property we're talking about here: there's someone living in the house and paying rent.

Let's go back to mortgage-lover Mandy, who has a 75% mortgage. The interest rate is 5%. It's an interest-only mortgage, meaning she pays the 5% interest each year and still owes the initial amount at the end.

Mandy's £75,000 mortgage will cost her £312.50 every month for ten years – that's £37,500 in total. As long as she's renting out the house for more than £312.50 plus running costs per month, she never has to pay a penny of it out of her own pocket: the rent from her tenant covers it all.

So she's just made a profit of £100,000 without paying any of the interest herself. Now do you see why most of the world's richest people got rich through property?

Too much of a good thing can be dangerous

So more leverage = better return on investment, right?

Right. But let's move the scenario on.

I forgot to mention that although the price of the house doubled over ten years, after the first two years it had actually dipped by 20%.

What if Dave, Mandy and Leon all lost their jobs after two years and needed the money they'd invested to live on? They'd each need to sell their house right away, but could only get £80,000 for it.

Dave didn't have any borrowing, so he can sell it for £80,000 and put the cash back in the bank. He's still lost £20,000, or 20% of his original investment.

Mandy's house is also worth £80,000, but she owes £75,000 on it. She sells the house, pays back the £75,000, and has only £5,000 left for herself. She's lost £20,000, just like Dave, but that's 80% of her original investment!

It's even worse for Leon though – his house is worth £80,000 but his outstanding loan is £90,000. This puts him in what's called "negative equity": selling the house won't be enough to clear the loan, so he's stuck – his cash is trapped in the property until its value increases. If for any reason he's unable to keep up his mortgage repayments (say the property was empty for a long period of time), he doesn't have the option of selling the property to solve the problem. He could end up having the house repossessed, losing 100% of his investment and leaving him unable to get credit in future.

So leverage works both ways: it multiplies potential gains, but also potential losses.

With great power...

A major tax change came fully into effect from April 2020, which has made the use of leverage less attractive – but not for everyone.

We'll come back to this in more detail later, but in the world's smallest nutshell…

From the time when buy-to-let first came into existence all the way up until April 2017, the interest you paid on your mortgage was considered to be a cost of doing business. So, if you rented a property out for £500, had mortgage payments of £300 and other costs of £100, you were left with a £100 taxable profit.

But starting in 2017 and fully in place by 2020, a new rule means that individuals can't deduct the mortgage payment as a cost of doing business before calculating their profit (although companies that own property still *can*).

In the example above, this means that your *taxable* profit becomes £400 (the £500 rent minus the £100 other costs), even though the money you've got left in the bank (what you'd think of as your "real" profit) is only £100. You can, however, claim an allowance against your tax bill equal to 20% of the interest payments.

If that makes sort-of sense, that's enough for now – we'll get into the full maths of the situation later.

The unintended consequence of this new rule is that it makes life very difficult for the authors of simple-and-breezy property books, because the exact same use of leverage now means different things for different property owners:

- Leverage is just as attractive for people who hold properties within limited companies, because they're not affected by the new rules.

- Leverage is *also* just as attractive for anyone whose earnings don't reach the higher rate threshold, because the new 20% allowance offsets the extra tax…

- … But because "taxable profit" is calculated earlier in the process, it means more people with property income will be pushed into the higher rate band.

- And anyone in the higher rate band – whether they were there already, or have been pushed there as a result of this change – will end up paying more.

How's a guy meant to crack a few jokes and keep it simple under these circumstances?

As I said, this is something we'll come back to. The general upshot, though, is that there's now a much greater need to think about the tax consequences before taking on a new mortgage – because if you're not careful, you could end up in a loss-making situation after taking tax into account.

For now… onwards!

So far we've only looked at one source of income for property investors: the capital growth that allows you to sell and cash in many multiples of what you've put in. We've ignored income – but we'll turn our attention to that in the next chapter.

Chapter 2
Growth vs income

Without the merest shadow of a doubt, the greatest property-related TV show of all time was Property Ladder.

In every episode we'd see a couple of utter pillocks buy a property at an over-inflated price, then undertake some kind of bonkers conversion or refurbishment. They'd be watched over by the perma-pregnant Sarah Beeny, who did her utmost to gently suggest that converting a two-bedroom semi in Grimsby into four high-end luxury shoeboxes might not be the best move, or that hot-pink textured walls aren't everyone's ideal decor.

Inevitably, after overrunning by six months and adding very little value, the pillocks would then sell their hot-pink high-end shoeboxes for a handsome profit – purely because the whole market had risen by about 40% in the time it took them to rip out a historic original fireplace.

Unfortunately, many viewers were interpreting it as a how-to guide: hey, if those idiots can do it, then I can too!

In retrospect, the whole show was the surest sign we had of the coming apocalypse: when total amateurs are diving into an unfamiliar industry, screwing everything up and still walking away with double-digit profits, it's high time for a serious market correction.

(When the correction came, a follow-up series called Property Snakes and Ladders showed what happened to the people who were still gaily ripping out load-bearing walls when the economic system collapsed. For some reason, Beeny wasn't knighted for her re-straint in never once laughing in their faces.)

Too much growth, not enough income

Anyway! The point is that during this boom/bubble, everyone was fixated on growth. In a market that's rising 25% every quarter, I suppose that's understandable.

But while growth is great, you can never be totally sure when (or to what extent) it will happen. If you're buying purely with growth in mind and the property isn't making you any money month on month, you're gambling that the capital value will rise before your monthly expenses increase and push you into a loss.

Rental income, on the other hand, isn't a gamble: you can pretty much lock it in when you buy, and collect it forever.

Say you put down £25,000 to buy a house worth £100,000. You then rent it out for £700 per month. An interest-only mortgage at 5% would cost you £312.50 per month. Let's budget £100 per month for repairs. What does that leave?

Two hundred and eighty seven pounds and fifty pence per month in pre-tax profit. Every month. Forever!

Of course, we've forgotten management fees. And any periods where you don't have a tenant. And the fact that your mortgage rate might go up. And that rents might go down. And tax. But you can build all that into your calculations.

The point is that if the property doesn't go up in value for a number of years – and even if it goes down for a bit – you've still got £287.50 dropping into your bank account every month.

Naturally, nobody wants the value of their property to go down – and historically, the gains investors have made from capital growth have dwarfed their rental returns. But given that you have no control over growth, you'd better make sure that the property is making you money every month.

Re-enter our old friend leverage

The use of leverage is, of course, a factor in whether or not the property makes you money every month – because the bigger the mortgage you take on, the more the interest payments are going to take a bite out of your monthly income. (And depending on your circumstances, the new tax treatment of mortgage interest might make that bite even bigger.)

During the last boom, people were taking on such massive mortgages that the property would actually *cost* them every month – and they didn't care, because its value was going up faster than they were having to put in money to pay the bills. I even know some landlords who *didn't bother putting tenants into their properties*, because it was less effort to just shovel in the cash while they watched the value rocket.

Clearly, this is madness.

Leverage, in short, is a great tool to help you benefit from rising prices – because at its simplest, it means you can buy (for example) four properties instead of one and therefore expose yourself to more capital growth. But at the same time, the interest payments make it harder for you to make a monthly profit.

Growth + income = happiness

Don't worry about manners: there's nothing wrong with being greedy and trying to get the best of both worlds. By all means target properties where you think there's the potential for growth, but make sure it's earning you an income whatever happens.

Even though you *can* and *should* have both growth and income, you'll normally have to make some sort of trade-off. For example, an extremely cheap terraced house in a struggling northern town will often give you a great return on investment, but it's unlikely to experience much in the way of growth. Conversely, you might think that a swanky flat in a trendy area of London has great growth potential, but you're likely to make less of a monthly return (even though the rent is higher) because it's so expensive to buy in the first place.

In short, although you want both, you'll need to plan your purchases with some kind of opinion as to which you want to optimise for.

Speaking of planning purchases… in order to start comparing properties against each other, we'll need some way of knowing which will give us the best return. We achieve that using a simple calculation called the *yield*, and that's the subject of the next chapter.

Chapter 3
Maths alert: Essential property calculations

If you've read anything about property, you'll have seen yield mentioned. But what exactly is it?

For our purposes, yield is nothing more complicated than the (pre-tax) return you get on an investment. So if you have your money in a savings account that pays you 5% interest, that's giving you a 5% yield. Yield is always expressed as a percentage.

So to calculate the yield, you just divide the return you get from an asset by the price of buying the asset.

In other words, if a house produces rent of £10,000 per year and it cost £200,000 to buy, 10,000 / 200,000 = 0.05.

We move the decimal point two places to the right to express that 0.05 as a percentage, so it's a 5% yield.

(An important note at this point: I've chosen my examples in this chapter to make the maths easy to follow – *not* because they're an accurate representative of the returns I aim to achieve.)

Who needs a yield?

You wouldn't want to base an investment decision solely on the yield, but it's a pretty neat place to start.

Firstly, the yield is a great way to compare the merits of different investments. For example, you're offered the opportunity to buy a house for £130,000 that generates £9,500 per year in rent, or a flat that costs £60,000 and brings in £6,000 per year in rent. All else being equal, which is the better investment?

Well, the yield of the house is 9,500 (the annual rent) divided by 130,000 (the purchase price), which is 0.073. Move the decimal point two places to the right so it's a percentage, which gives you 7.3%.

The yield of the flat is 6,000 / 60,000, which is 10%. So while there will be many other factors, the flat is the best investment purely in terms of return.

You can also work backwards: have a target yield in mind, and use it to work out how much you should be paying to acquire an asset.

So if there's a flat that I know will rent for £12,000 and I'm hell bent on getting a 10% yield, I can multiply the rent by the percentage yield (£12,000 x 10) and know that I can't pay a penny more than £120,000 to buy the flat. If it's being marketed for £200,000, I'm gonna pass.

Gross yield, net yield...

When people talk about yield, they normally mean exactly what we've been talking about. It's also known as the **gross yield**.

The gross yield is useful for making comparisons, but you absolutely don't want to make an investment based purely on it. That's because you haven't taken your costs into account.

When I was using gross yield to determine whether to buy the house or the flat just now, that wasn't really the right tool for the job – because a house and a flat have different ownership costs associated with them.

So while gross yield is a handy shortcut to compare properties that are likely to have similar running costs, you'll want to work out the **net yield** to get more precise.

Net yield just means the return once all your costs have been deducted. It's more effort to calculate, but gives a more accurate idea of the true return you'll see on your investment.

That flat I mentioned, which brings in annual rent of £12,000? Let's say I drove a hard bargain and managed to buy it for £120,000. That's a 10% gross yield – pretty good!

But that doesn't mean I get to put all that rental income in the bank:

- My interest-only mortgage costs me £375 per month, or £4,500 per year.

- I give 10% of my annual rental income, or £1,200, to my letting agent.

- I budget 10% (or £1,200) of my annual rent for repairs.

- As it's a flat, there's a service charge of £600 per year that I have to pay.

- I should probably factor in a loss of income through voids (the property sitting empty between tenants), but as there's no way of knowing in advance what it'll be, everyone has to use their own judgement to decide how much to estimate. Let's leave voids aside for now.

Once all those expenses are deducted from the £12,000 rent, I'm left with £4,500 in annual profit.

If I divide that £4,500 by the purchase price of £120,000, I get a net yield of 3.75%.

Wow – that's a long way from 10%. At that kind of level I might consider just investing in the stock market instead, and saving myself from ever having to talk to an estate agent or lawyer.

Ah, but I'm forgetting something: I didn't put in all of the cash to buy the flat... I got a mortgage.

Return on investment (ROI)

Remember my interest-only mortgage that costs £375 per month? That's because I borrowed 75% of the property's value, or £90,000, in order to buy it.

I only put in £30,000 of my own cash.

So what's my return on my own investment? Well, I already know how much profit I have after deducting all expenses: £4,500 per year. So I just need to divide my annual profit by the amount of money I invested myself.

That's £4,500 / £30,000, which equals a 15% return on investment. Suddenly those unpleasant encounters with estate agents and lawyers all seem worthwhile.

(For the simplicity of explaining the concept, I've not factored costs like stamp duty, surveys and legal fees into my "investment" number. These are real costs that need to be paid upfront, so you should add them to the "amount of money invested" when running your own calculations.)

This is our old friend leverage again: borrowing 75% of the money quadrupled my return on investment compared to if I'd put up all the money myself.

Which of these numbers actually matter?

All of the numbers we've looked at have got some value for you as a property investor:

- The gross yield lets you directly compare competing investments.

- The net yield shows the return you'll get after factoring in all costs.

- Your return on investment (ROI) shows how hard your money is working for you.

For me, ROI is the ultimate number: it tells you exactly what return you're getting on your cash, so you can even compare it with the returns you'd get in non-property investments.

Increasing your returns

Now that we know how yield is calculated, it's clear there are only two ways to end up with a higher **net yield**:

- Buy cheaper

- End up with more rental profit

Buying cheaper is the single best thing you can do: it makes a big difference to your yield, and builds lots of healthy equity for you into the bargain. In other words, if you buy a property for £80,000 when it's actually worth £100,000, you'll be making the same rental return with less outlay – while also giving yourself "instant equity" of £20,000.

But as well as buying cheaper, there are lots of ways to improve the other part of the equation – making more rental profit:

- You can refurbish to try to bring in more rent... but that will involve investing more cash at the start.

- You can rent out each room individually to sharers rather than a single family... but that might increase your maintenance costs.

- You can save about 10% by cutting out the letting agent and doing it yourself... but that's a hassle, and the cost of your own time needs to be factored in.

So you can increase your net yield by buying cheaper or reducing costs, but you can also increase your **return on investment** by putting in less of your own funds. If you borrow a higher percentage of the purchase price, you'll need to put in less of your own cash – and your ROI will therefore go up. This will need to be balanced against tax and risk considerations though, as we'll come to later.

At its root, investment is just finding a way to achieve your financial targets by playing around with different options to find the one that suits you best. And the number of variables you can fiddle with – both human and numerical – are what makes property investment such a fascinating thing to be involved in.

Now... you've probably noticed that these calculations only address one of the two factors we were trying to balance in the last chapter: income, not growth. That's because – while we may buy with growth in mind –

there's no surefire way of predicting what that growth will be or when it will come.

Some people (normally when they're trying to sell you something) will assume a capital growth rate of (say) 5% per year, and include that as part of your "total return". Growth isn't something to forget about, but to me it makes no sense to bake assumed growth into your model: it implies that something is definitely going to happen, when the only certainty is that it won't happen to the exact extent and timescale you've predicted.

Chapter 4
Stacking a deal

Now that we've run through the basic principles, you're *almost* ready to get onto Rightmove, do some ooh-ing and aah-ing over the lovely stuff you can buy, and run some of them through your new calculations to see how much money (if any) they'll make you.

Of course, the numbers you come up with are only as good as the data you put in – so in this chapter, we'll look at the typical costs you're likely to encounter in the course of buying a property. We'll need to look at:

- The upfront purchase costs of buying the property (your "investment").

- Calculating the rent it can generate, which can be paired with the upfront costs to calculate gross yield.

- The running costs, which you need to deduct from the rent to calculate your net yield or ROI.

Purchase costs

The property itself

Yes, the biggest purchase cost will of course be the property itself. It's going to be obvious what the cost actually *is* once you've paid it, but let's digress for a moment to discuss how to calculate what you *should* be paying. In other words, what is the property actually worth?

The "market value" of a property is essentially whatever someone is willing to pay for it – literally, the value that the market puts on the property. Imagine, however, that you're selling a house at 66 London Road, and next door (number 64) is also on sale – both for £500,000. One day a particularly superstitious oligarch decides he wants to move to the area, and his lucky number is 66 – so he immediately offers you £1 million to make sure he doesn't miss out. (Clearly this is a silly exaggeration, but because property is an emotional purchase there are any number of reasons why someone would "overpay" by some margin.)

A happy turn of events for you, but it doesn't mean that the house is suddenly worth £1 million – nor that the house next door is suddenly worth £1 million either. It was just a random stroke of luck. For that reason, we need a more reliable way of assessing value.

When a professional surveyor is valuing a property, they'll take into account the sale price of:

- Similar properties (so they're comparing like with like), that are…

- Nearby (because location obviously affects price), and have…

- Sold recently (because the whole market moves over time)

They'll disregard any outliers (like our oligarch's impulse buy), and also disregard *asking* prices – all that matters is what similar, nearby properties actually sold for. When you're assessing a property, you can do exactly the same thing: go to Rightmove and select "Sold house prices", and all the historic data is there.

It's easiest when you know an area well, of course, because you'll know that (for example) two-bedroom houses on one street tend to be bigger than those on the next street and would therefore be worth slightly more. Even without that knowledge though, you'll be able to get reasonably close.

It should go without saying that the market value of the property has exactly *nothing* to do with the asking price. Some asking prices are more realistic than others, but as far as possible it's best to just put it out of your mind and stick to the facts.

Stamp duty

As part of "the great warning off of 2015", which I talked about back at the start, our esteemed chancellor hit us with a nasty extra cost: higher rates of stamp duty for investors than for owner-occupiers. I won't put the actual rates here in case they all change again, but if you search for "stamp duty rates 2021" they'll come up.

The upshot is that investors must pay rates that are 3% higher than the "normal" rates. For very expensive properties in the South East this can make a massive difference, but it also adds expense at the other end of the market. The 0% band that previously extended up to £125,000 has become a 3% band, which means a cost of an extra few thousand pounds for even the cheapest typical investment purchases.

There's not a lot that can be done about it, so just bake it into your figures.

Legal fees

Unless you're a total masochist (or a solicitor), you'll need a solicitor to handle the purchase on your behalf. Fees depend on the value of the property, as well as factors like whether it's freehold or leasehold (because leasehold properties require more things to be checked) and whether they're also dealing with paperwork relating to a mortgage.

On top of the actual fees, you'll need to budget another couple of hundred for the various "searches" they need to request and check over. If you're buying the property as a company, you can expect to pay more because there's more paperwork for the solicitor to deal with.

This is *not* an area to try to cut costs: the standard of service that solicitors provide is variable (to put it nicely), so it's not worth deviating from a trusted recommendation to save a few hundred pounds.

Survey fees

If you're getting a mortgage, the lender will insist on doing their own survey – which you'll have to pay for. This is just a perfunctory valuation to make sure it's worth as much as you claim it is, and they won't look in any detail at the structure of the building itself.

You might decide to fork out for your own survey too. The most appropriate survey for anything other than very old or specialist properties is a HomeBuyer Report, which will flag up any causes for concern in aspects like the structure, drainage, heating, damp and so on. The cost again depends on the value of the property, but I've paid in the range of £300–500 in the past.

Should you bother with a survey? For flats I don't, because they normally can't get access to areas like the roof and communal heating – which are the biggest potential costs. For houses it's probably worth it to cover yourself – but annoyingly, it can mean more money down the drain if the deal falls through.

Finance fees

If you're taking out a mortgage to buy the property, you're going to fork out for a product fee, a valuation fee, possibly some other fees just for the fun of it, and a broker fee if someone helps to arrange it for you.

The product fee can normally be added to the loan rather than paid upfront; it's helpful for cashflow, but still very much a real cost.

Achievable rent

We've already established that you can't predict capital growth with any degree of accuracy – but you *can* get very close to the mark when it comes to rental income.

Just like when it comes to establishing market value, the market *rental* value is determined by what similar properties nearby are currently available for. There's a common belief that landlords can (and do) charge whatever they feel like, but it's just not true – as you'll find out if you overprice the rent and watch your property languish on the market for weeks.

So, take a look on a portal like Rightmove to see what nearby properties of equivalent size and condition are being marketed for. You can tick a box to include "let agreed" properties in the results, but you'll still only know the rent that was being *asked* and not the sum that was eventually *agreed*. It doesn't really matter, because (unlike properties for sale) rents don't tend to get negotiated by massive amounts. If you really want to know what properties ended up renting for, you'll be surprised how much you can find out by calling a letting agent and just asking.

Running costs

Mortgage payments

We'll take a closer look at mortgages in the next chapter, but the payments you make (if you choose to use a mortgage at all) will almost certainly be your largest running cost.

Maintenance

When it comes to maintenance costs, one's thing for certain: you'll have a few to pay.

And that's where the certainty ends. Will the boiler blow up on day one or soldier on for ten years? Will a mystery leak spring up in the middle of the night and damage the floor? Nobody knows – and you won't know how the costs average out until you've owned a property for a few years.

My rule of thumb used to be to budget 10% of the rent for houses and 5% for flats, but I retired it when I realised that it varied so widely it was pretty much meaningless. Instead, I just keep a healthy cash reserve to make sure I can cover whatever costs come along.

Even if you don't formally budget a certain amount in your numbers, there's a certainty you'll have some degree of maintenance costs to meet – so your potential returns won't be as high in reality as they are on your spreadsheet.

Service charge/ground rent

If you're buying a flat, there'll be a service charge and ground rent to pay. You'll need to find out how much they cost right at the start of your research into a property: charges seem to bear little relation to the services received, and they can make a massive difference to your returns.

Some people swear off flats because you have so little control over service charges, but if the numbers still add up it doesn't bother me – and the upside is that there's so much less maintenance to worry about.

Insurance

As a minimum, you'll need to take out buildings in-surance. It's a condition of any mortgage – and even if you own the property outright, it's not worth accept-ing even the smallest risk of your house burning down and leaving you with nothing. On top of buildings insurance, you can choose to insure your contents – such as any carpets and kitchen appliances you provide. (It's always the tenant's responsibility to insure their own possessions.)

The cost of insurance depends largely on the "rebuild value" of the property (the maximum it would cost the insurer if the property burned to the ground and they had to pay for it to be re-built from scratch), with a whole host of other smaller factors playing into the premium you end up getting charged.

Voids

At some point, your property will be empty – whether that's because you can't find tenants, or because you need a short gap between tenancies to do a bit of up-keep.

This "lost rent" is a cost, so it makes sense to budget it in rather than pretend you're going to get 52 weeks of rent out of every year. Something between two weeks and a month is probably realistic. A city-centre flat could conceivably change occupants once per year with a two-week gap; a three-bedroom house might only turn over once every few years but take a bit longer to find the perfect tenants.

Bills

If you include any bills as part of the rent, this is obviously a cost. As a rule, bills only tend to be included in properties rented out by the room.

Adding it up

While not an exhaustive list of every cost, those are the main ones I use when establishing the gross yield, net yield and ROI of any given investment – I just put together a basic spreadsheet where I tap in the numbers and it spits out the results.

I might need to hand in my Geek badge at some point, because I've seen plenty of spreadsheets that are infinitely more elaborate and pretty much get down to the cost of a postage stamp for sending the signed contract back to the solicitor. For me though, given that there are so many assumptions that are bound to be wrong anyway (like an allowance for voids and maintenance), I don't see the point in going overboard. If it's a good investment, it should be obvious without having to account for every last theoretical penny.

Chapter 5
Mortgages

WARNING: Taking out a mortgage is a big frickin' deal. This is not the kind of thing you want to take advice about from some guy in a book. Although (spoiler alert) at the end I tell you to talk to a mortgage broker. You should take that bit of advice.

If you own your own home already, you'll have it on a residential mortgage. That means the lender has given you the money based on you living there, they trust that your income will be sufficient to make your re-payments, and you can't rent it out to anyone else (unless you get their permission).

When you're renting out a property to someone else though, you need a buy-to-let (BTL) mortgage. For this, the lender will consider the likely rental income as well as your personal income when deciding if they'll lend you the money. Shortly, we'll look at all the factors that lenders consider.

(Very very important note: Don't be tempted to try letting a property on a residential mortgage without anyone noticing. This often happens if someone starts renting out the place where they used to live and doesn't inform their lender. You might think that as long as they're getting their money each month, the lenders won't notice or care, but it's mortgage fraud and they can immediately revoke your loan when they find out.)

Interest only vs repayment

In the examples we've looked at so far, we've always used an interest-only mortgage. As the name implies, you're just paying the interest as a fee for being allowed to borrow the money – and at the end of the mortgage term, you'll still owe the exact same amount you borrowed to start with.

In investment, that's by far the most common way of doing things. At the end of the mortgage term you repay the amount you borrowed by selling the property, or taking out another mortgage, or paying it off with the vast wads of cash you've accumulated in the meantime.

By contrast, when you buy a house to live in, you'll usually take out a capital repayment mortgage. That means that over the course of the mortgage term (often 25 years), you'll gradually pay off the entire amount you borrowed *in addition* to the interest. That makes capital repayment mortgages more expensive than if you were paying the interest only, but there's a huge upside: at the end, the house is 100% yours.

Capital repayment is great for your own residence, because when it's paid off you get to live in it cost-free for the rest of your life, and pass it on to your kids. For investment purposes, though, you need to consider your overall strategy before deciding whether or not to repay the capital.

For example, if you're borrowing £100,000 over 25 years at a 5% rate of interest:

- The monthly payment for the interest only would be £416.66.

- The monthly payment for interest + repayment would be £591.27.

For that reason, interest-only is often the only option: by the time you've paid for maintenance, a letting agent, insurance and everything else that goes along with owning a buy-to-let property, you'd often end up making a loss if you tried to pay off the capital too.

A wonderful thing about interest-only mortgages is that while it doesn't look like you're making a dent in the amount you've borrowed, inflation will erode the *real* value of the money you owe.

For example, let's say that in 2010 you borrowed £75,000 to buy a house for £100,000. By 2020, if your house had just gone up in line with inflation, it would be worth £136,000 – but you still only owe £75,000. That means that without any repayments of the capital, your loan-to-value ratio has gone from 75% to 55%.

Many investors therefore let inflation work its magic, put their extra cash into more purchases rather than repayments, and don't worry about paying off the debt until years and years into the future. But it depends on your investment strategy: some investors find that it suits their objectives better to start making a dent in the debt pile immediately.

There's no fits-all answer as to which is best, but you'd have to put together one heck of a persuasive argument to talk me out of using interest-only mortgages for my own portfolio. The point that a lot of people miss is that an interest-only loan doesn't mean that you *can't* pay off the capital – just that you're not locked into a repayment schedule to do so. For me, it's the best of both worlds: I get the extra cashflow every month, and every so often I can decide whether to use that cash in the bank to pay down debt or expand my portfolio.

Will banks lend to you?

You've found a property and you've had an offer accepted… so now it's time to see if you can get a mortgage to buy it, right?

WRONG! You want to be looking into mortgages well in advance – before you waste your time and put your reputation at risk by finding out that you can't follow through with a purchase. Lenders want to know about you as a person as well as the property you're planning to buy, and you might need to do some advance preparation to make yourself more creditworthy.

You

The ideal client for a mortgage lender would look something like this:

- Owns their own residential home

- Earns more than £25,000 as an employee (*not* income from property)

- Is resident in the UK

- Has a squeaky-clean credit history

- Has an investment property or two already, but not too many

If you tick all those boxes, you'll have the majority of lenders available to you. The further you depart from the ideal, the more lenders will drop out of the running – leaving you with a smaller choice, and probably higher rates and fees to reflect their extra risk.

Don't tick every box? Don't worry, because a lot of people don't. It's worth speaking to a mortgage adviser early, to find out what your options are and if there's anything you can do to boost your chances of getting accepted by more lenders.

The property

Mortgage lenders don't just want to know about *you* – they're pretty interested in the property they'll be lending against, too.

Lenders tend not to like:

- Very cheap properties, where the loan would be less than £40,000 (because it's just not worth their while).

- Non-standard construction, like concrete or wood.

- Properties that aren't habitable at the point of the loan being made (even if you're going to sort it out later), such as there being no adequate kitchen or bathroom.

- Flats above shops.

- Anything with a short lease.

The proposed tenant type comes into it too. Some lenders won't accept students, or people on benefits. If you're renting the property to multiple people who aren't related, lenders will rule themselves in or out on the basis of whether they're on the same contract or individual tenancies, whether the bedroom doors have locks, and so on.

Because every lender has their own criteria about both the borrower and the property, sometimes these over-lap to make life particularly difficult for people just starting out. For example, one lender might accept four students sharing a house on individual tenancies… but only if you're not a first-time landlord. That's why you should get advice early, because it might be the case that the type of purchase you had in mind will be a real struggle given your current status.

How much can you borrow?

So a lender is happy with you and the property you're planning to buy. Now… how much cash are they going to slip your way so you can seal the deal without scrambling down the back of too many sofas?

The total amount you can borrow will come down to two factors: the loan-to-value ratio, and rental cover.

Loan-to-value

As we've already seen, lenders will offer you a certain percentage of the purchase price – known as the loan-to-value (LTV) ratio. While 75% is typical, there *are* some 80% products and even the odd 85% product out there. Once you drop below 60%, you'll tend to get cheaper rates to reflect the lower risk.

Once you've had an offer accepted and made your mortgage application, the lender will send out a surveyor to assess its value based on local "comparables". All being well, they'll assess its value at the same amount you agreed to pay (it will never be higher). If the surveyor thinks you're paying too much (or just had an argument with his wife that morning), the property could be "down-valued" – meaning they'll only lend (for example) 75% of the *lower* value they've put on the property. Such a scenario leaves you with three choices: you can put in more money yourself, or try to negotiate a lower price with the vendor, or pull out of the deal entirely.

Rental cover

The lender needs to be convinced that the rental income will be sufficient to cover the mortgage payment, and they use a measure called "rental cover" to assess this.

The minimum that any lender will require is "125% rental cover" at a 5.5% interest rate, meaning that the rent is at least 25% higher than your monthly mortgage payment – and assuming that you're paying 5.5% rather than your current rate, to give some headroom for rates going up. For example:

- You're borrowing £100,000 on an interest-only basis

- The monthly repayment at a 5.5% interest rate (regardless of what you're actually paying) will be £458

- The rent needs to be at least £572.50 per month (£458 x 1.25)

At the same time as valuing the property, the surveyor will give their opinion as to the amount of rent it can achieve – and this can be "down-valued" too, which might affect the amount you can borrow.

Each lender has slightly different rental cover requirements. For example, some want 135% or 145% rather than 125%. Others will vary their requirements depending on your other sources of income or your tax bracket.

So while the loan-to-value sets out the maximum amount you can borrow, it could be reduced by the rental cover requirement.

Choosing the best product

When it comes to choosing the right mortgage product, then, you need to first narrow it down to the lenders where you and the proposed property both meet their criteria. But the fun is only just beginning, because you'll also want to look at:

- The interest rate

- Whether to go for a variable or a fixed rate – and if fixed, for how long?

- The arrangement fee

- The valuation and legal fees

- If there are any penalties for overpayments or early redemption

- Any nasty terms or restrictions

… And about a million other things. Because I have better things to do with my time than look into all this boring stuff (like, erm, sitting around *writing* about all this boring stuff), I pay a mortgage broker to do it for me. And you probably should too.

Clearly, there's more to picking the right product than just seeing who appears at the top of a "best buy" table for having the lowest headline rate. I do know investors who go through all the small print themselves and work out what's best, but I really don't understand why they bother. A broker won't just find the right product for you – they'll also submit the application on your behalf and make sure it goes through, saving you yet more time and stress in answering any questions the lender asks.

All brokers will get paid a fee by the lender for "introducing" you, and some also charge the client (that's you) for their services. A typical fee is somewhere around £500, and I have no problem paying this: if I'm paying, my assumption is that the broker will need to take on less business to make the same amount of money, so I'll get a better service.

Whatever you do though, don't just walk into the high street branch of whoever you bank with. Their in-house adviser will only be able to offer you choices from their own product range... and with so many factors in play, it's unlikely that they'll have the best product on the market for your exact situation.

Chapter 6
Tax

When someone's determined to be sceptical about property investment, their response to just about any argument seems to be: "But… tax!"

And, yes – you'll need to pay some. (As we know, the only other certainties are death and the phone ringing just as you sit down to dinner.) Rather than letting it scare you off though, what matters is to understand the impact tax will have – so you can decide whether property is still worth the effort after paying it, or if you're better off investing in other asset classes.

How property tax works

If you think of property investment as a business (even if you just own properties in your own name), you'll already understand how the taxation of property works: you make revenue (rental income), you incur expenses, and you pay tax on what's left over after those expenses. Easy. (With the exception that the genuine expense of mortgage interest now *isn't* an allowable expense when it comes to tax, as we'll cover shortly.)

With properties owned in your own name, the profits are added to any other sources of income, and you pay income tax on the total. So if you earn £40,000 from your job and make a £10,000 profit from property, you'll pay income tax on the total of £50,000.

If instead you buy the properties within the structure of a limited company, you'll pay corporation tax on the profits. On the face of it that seems better for higher earners, because corporation tax is lower than the higher rates of income tax. But if you want the company to pay you the profits so you can spend them, you'll need to take those profits as wages or dividends and be taxed accordingly.

Then, when you come to sell the property, there will be capital gains tax to pay on the difference between the purchase price (plus associated costs) and the sale price.

Capital vs revenue expenses

From a tax point-of-view, your expenditure falls into two different categories:

- "Running costs" (maintenance, agency fees, insurance), which you can deduct from your rental income as you go along (known as "revenue" expenses).

- "Purchase costs" (the property itself, stamp duty, legal fees), which you can only deduct from the sale price when you eventually sell (known as "capital" expenses).

Capital expenses are annoying, because you can only claim them in the distant future when (or if) you eventually sell – by which point inflation will mean that the £300 invoice for a survey that you've diligently filed for 20 years will save you the cost of a Mars bar if you're lucky.

Revenue expenses, however, are great (as far as an expense can be great) because they reduce your tax bill as you go along. You obviously don't want to incur unnecessary costs to save a bit of tax, but you *do* want to keep good records so you don't forget to deduct any legitimate costs.

What constitutes a legitimate cost? Just about everything after the point of buying the property: repairs, letting agent fees, service charges, ground rent, any bills you're liable for while the property is empty... all the way down to the cost of relevant phone calls and postage costs, if you really want to reclaim every penny.

Hang on though – I didn't mention the cost of your mortgage in there. And that's where things get a little more complicated...

Mortgage interest tax relief

Back when we were talking about leverage, I touched on some changes to mortgage interest costs that took effect in April 2017.

In a nutshell:

- Previously, your interest payments were a cost of doing business (a "revenue" cost) like any other. They could be deducted from your income before arriving at your profit.

- Since April 2020, interest payments aren't an allowable cost for individuals – so you calculate your profits as if you haven't incurred any interest costs at all. Then, you can deduct 20% of your interest costs from the tax you owe.

- In the years between April 2017 and April 2020, investors applied part of their interest costs under the old method and the rest under the new one. The proportions gradually shifted over the three years to phase it in.

- For companies, none of this applies and you just carry on as before.

Let's take a look at how the "old" and "new" methods actually work. For example, for an individual as it stood before April 2017:

(£10,000 rental income) - (£5,000 mortgage interest) - (£1,000 other costs) = £4,000 profit. Income tax at 20% would be £800, and at 40% would be £1,600.

And today:

(£10,000 rental income) - (£1,000 other costs) = £9,000 profit. Relief can be claimed on the £5,000 mortgage interest at 20%, which is £1,000.

If you're a basic rate taxpayer, you therefore pay income tax of 20% on the £9,000 profit (£1,800), *minus* the £1,000. That leaves you with £800 – just like before. If you're a higher rate taxpayer, income tax of 40% on the £9,000 profit gets you to £3,600, *minus* the £1,000 – leaving you with a tax bill of £2,600.

As you can see, the upshot is that those whose income falls entirely within the basic rate threshold are unaffected because the 20% allowance offsets the extra tax, while everyone else ends up paying more tax to some extent. However, "profits" are now higher for everyone (because you can't deduct your interest costs before arriving at them), so more people will be pushed into the higher rate band.

Is this an argument for buying properties within a company to avoid the whole issue? In a way, yes. But in a way, also no:

- Companies don't have a capital gains tax allowance, so end up paying more tax when selling a property.

- If you pay tax at the higher rate and you want to actually take the profits out of the company, you'll probably end up paying *more* tax by the time you've been taxed on the dividends too. (If you just leave the profits building up within the company to buy the next property, that's not an issue.)

- There are extra accountancy costs for companies.

- Borrowing for companies tends to come with higher costs.

So there's no "right" answer. If, though, you're looking for a very general rule of thumb (which certainly isn't tax advice), try this: when investors have income falling within the higher rate band *and* they're happy to leave profits building up (instead of spending them), they often find themselves better off buying within a company.

It depends on a multitude of factors, though, so the only *real* answer is to consult an accountant if you're in any doubt. But first, let's take a deep breath and put all this tax stuff into perspective.

A bit of perspective

You'll hear people talking about the restriction of finance cost relief as if it's the end of days for property investors. For some people with large, highly leveraged portfolios that weren't generating much profit, it actually has been.

But if you're just getting into the game now, do calculate the effect that tax will have on your returns but definitely don't freak out about it. For me, the effect of the changes was about £500 per property per year. I'd rather not pay that, but does it destroy the entire concept of investing in property? Of course not.

And I think that's the overall message about tax in general: don't freak out. People tend to get very emotional about this subject and hate giving any of their hard-earned cash away (usually while insisting loudly that everyone else should have to give away more of theirs, but that's another issue), and lose sight of reality. Keep good records so you can claim every legitimate expense you can, then do your best to hand over the required chunk of profits with good grace. Or at least without bawling and making a scene.

Now that we've covered a lot of the basics, you should have a decent idea of the things you ought to be thinking about as an investor:

- Should you invest for income or growth?

- How can yield calculations help you weigh up competing investment opportunities?

- How much leverage should you use to super-charge your returns without an unacceptable level of risk?

- What type of mortgage should you take out?

Next, we'll move on to talking about strategy: how to set goals and work out how to achieve them, and a lot more besides.

PART 2:
DEVELOPING AN INVESTMENT STRATEGY

Chapter 7
Setting property investment goals

Before we move into specific strategies, we need to think about goals.

Why? Because there are probably tens of "bargain" property deals within a mile of where you are, which you could rush out and buy. But each property will have different strengths, attract a different target market, and drag you in a different direction.

Without goals, you'll end up owning a rag-tag bunch of properties that might not get you where you need to be.

What is a goal?

A goal is a dream with a deadline. "I want to own ten properties" is a dream; "I want to own ten properties by the time I'm 40" is a goal.

A goal is specific. "I want to be rich" is too vague and subjective to even know when you've achieved it. "I want to have a monthly income of £5,000 from property in three years' time" is more like it.

A goal should be ambitious. A goal of owning one property within five years isn't going to get you far (unless that's genuinely all you want). An ambitious goal will drive you forward, and even if you don't quite hit it you'll still have come a long way.

A goal is personal. Comparing your goals with other people's isn't going to be helpful. If you're in debt, an ambitious goal might be "I'll have saved up enough for a deposit within three years." If you've got bucket-loads of equity in your own house that you can release to invest, you'll need to work harder to stretch yourself.

A goal needs sub-goals. An ambitious goal might seem so scary and ridiculous you don't know where to start. But by breaking it down into sub-goals with shorter deadlines, you'll soon be able to see how you're making steps towards your overall goal.

Imagine your dream lifestyle, and set your goals to get you there

Property goals are about more than just money: you can set your course in any number of different ways to get to the lifestyle you want:

- If you want to keep your job and invest for a pension or a bit of extra income, you might just want one or two quality properties with strong rental demand.

- If you're never happier than when you're tinkering and DIYing, you might want to build a big portfolio that you can self-manage.

- If you view property as purely a means to an end and want to spend as much of your time as possible on the beach, you might want to aim for a small number of high cashflowing properties, and outsource the management.

- If you want to benefit from high yield and strong demand (and are willing to accept the

downsides), you might want to look at properties for tenants who are receiving benefits.

Your dream lifestyle will involve money, but how
much? If you're going to keep your job, your income
requirement will be very different from someone who
wants to spend their days in a hammock.

Do you need an income target or an equity target?

Depending on your goal, you might want to focus
mainly on either income or equity.

For example, if your goal is to replace your income
from your job over the next five years, you'll want to
focus on income. Just take your wage, work out how
much money you can make from each property per
month, and work out the number of properties you
need to replace your wage with rental income. That's
your goal.

But that might not motivate you. You might be motivated by the idea of having a certain amount of equity
in your portfolio – the magic £1 million, say – so you
know that when you retire in the future you can cash

it in and have a big lump sum in your bank account. That's good too.

Alternatively, you might want to quit your job *now* and immediately make as much money from property in a year as you were making as an employee. That probably won't be possible with just one property, but you could make your entire annual wage in one transaction if you buy a cheap property at auction, add value and sell it on.

Deciding whether to focus on income or equity will depend on your goal, and will have a large impact on the approach you choose.

Write down your goal and keep it in mind

Don't worry, I'm not going to ask you to visualise your success or ask the universe to send you what you want. But just think about your goal, and put it in writing. Make sure it's specific, ambitious, personal, has a deadline, and has sub-goals to serve as a road map to get you to where you need to be.

Chapter 8
Building a portfolio with limited funds

After reading Part 1 and giving some thought to your goals, you're probably thinking something along the lines of:

"OK, I get the difference between income and growth. I'm a total leverage fanboy. I've even dug out my abacus and got my head around the important calculations. But how the henry heckings am I ever going to afford to buy more than one property? I'm never going to have enough of a deposit to get the properties I need to achieve my goals."

It's a fair point: if you invest £25,000 to buy a property worth £100,000 and it nets you £300 in profit per month, that's great and everything... but it's not going to change your life. Unless the market value of your property increases and allows you to refinance (which you have no control over), you need to save up *another* £25,000 to buy the next one.

As the word "investment" rather gives away, property investment requires putting in money whichever way you slice it. As a smart investor, though, you can find ways to reuse your original investment to minimise the amount of cash you need to put into each new property – and it's worth running through those ways now, to give you the confidence that hitting your lofty targets *is* possible.

Broadly, there are two methods you can use to recycle your initial deposit: buying below market value, and adding *extra* value. Both involve "building in" additional equity, which you can tap into later.

We'll first look at what each of these methods involves, then tackle how to use them to fund future purchases.

Buy below market value (BMV)

Buying below market value (BMV) sounds like a brilliant idea – but who in their right mind would sell you anything for less than it's worth?

The answer is "motivated sellers" – a somewhat euphemistic term to describe people whose circumstances are forcing them to sell at a lower price, because they don't have time to wait for the best offer. Death, divorce and financial pressures are the usual causes.

It isn't common to find genuinely big discounts to market value through estate agents. You need to remember that *market value* is what matters: a discount of 20% from the asking price is no discount at all if the asking price was 20% too high to start with.

There's a perception that auctions are the place to look for a bargain, but their popularity in recent years (due in part to Homes Under The Hammer, I'm sure) has made this less true. If lots of people are looking at the same opportunity, the bidding will naturally approach the market value minus the value of any work needed, with a bit of a profit buffer in between.

Both of these methods *can* throw up great deals, however – and there are investors who've made a career out of finding seemingly "impossible" deals that have been under everyone else's nose the whole time.

If you can't find good discounts through agents or auctions, there are other methods – such as directly putting leaflets through doors offering to buy someone's house quickly. Many investors spend tens of thousands of pounds a year using these direct marketing methods – and make their money back many times over through the deals they unearth – but it takes concerted effort, and isn't something you can just dabble in.

However you go about it, discounts in the 25–30% range are extremely difficult to come by – especially in a buoyant market. Even if you could just secure a 10-15% discount though, it will still speed up your acquisition process: it means only needing to find roughly half as much cash to put into the next deal as you otherwise would have done.

Add value through refurbishment

If you can't buy cheap, the other way to recycle some of your deposit is to add value. Often, it's easier to get the result you want by combining the two: buy for 10% below market value then add 15% to the value through refurbishment, for example.

How do you add value? Well, the biggest ways to add value are by:

- Adding square footage

- Doing major refurbishment

- Solving a problem (usually legal) that has been restricting the value

Whichever method you use, the advantage is that you can often refinance the property at its full value (to free up cash) in a matter of months rather than years. If you've just negotiated a bargain but not done any work, you'll struggle to convince a valuer it's worth more than you paid for it – but if improvements of some kind have been made, this is a much easier case to make.

Adding square footage

Adding useful square footage is a sure-fire way to add value. Normally that's done by building an extension, adding a loft conversion, or digging out a basement.

Each of these options have different costs associated with them and add varying amounts of value. Bolting on a conservatory is relatively cheap, for example, but won't add all that much value. At the other end of the scale, adding a basement can add a lot of value (especially if you can create a separate basement flat out of it), but costs a bomb too.

Whenever you're considering the option of adding square footage, you need to be aware of the need for planning permission: if your investment strategy hinges on converting the loft but the local council is unlikely to approve your plans, you'd better think again. The housing section of the local authority's website is the place to find out.

Doing major refurbishment

While a fresh coat of magnolia and a few Glade plug-ins might be enough to add value in the eyes of a casual buyer, surveyors are a (rightly) more cynical sort. In order to get them to value the property significantly higher than it was when you bought it, you'll need to do some pretty major refurbishment.

A prime candidate would be a property that hadn't been updated since the 1970s, and subsequently had someone break in and nick the boiler and all the copper piping. Bringing that back up to scratch would certainly be enough to demonstrate that you've added value – although of course, you need to make sure that you're adding value over and above the money you've spent on the refurbishment.

The key to getting a surveyor to recognise the full value you've added is to show them "before and after" photos of the property, along with a full schedule of all the works. Without this evidence they'll have no idea what you've done, so will naturally assume that it's in the same condition as when you bought it and is therefore worth the same as you paid for it.

Solving legal problems

Legal issues are complicated and a non-expert like me can't talk about them in any great detail, but they can be a great way of adding value without spending much money if you know what you're doing.

Some ways that purely legal means can add value would include:

- Extending a short lease

- Taking over the freehold of a previously lease-hold property

- Successfully applying for a change of use (from commercial to residential, for example)

- Removing a restrictive covenant

- Being granted planning permission for future work

With the only costs being time and legal fees, spotting an opportunity that others have missed can be very lucrative.

However you do it, a fundamental part of property investment lies in minimising how much of your own cash you tie up. Just think back to the concept of return on investment (ROI): if you're using the same money over and over again to buy more and more houses, your ROI is theoretically infinite! That's pretty powerful stuff.

Tapping into the value

Having created an "equity cushion" by buying BMV or adding value (or a combination of the two), you can then tap into that equity. This is achieved by *refinancing*, to turn the equity into cash – then using the cash to buy your next property.

Confused? Don't be! Here's how it works…

Let's say you spot a property that you're sure is worth £200,000, but the vendor is in a rush to sell and they're willing to accept £150,000 for it.

If you need a mortgage to buy the property, the lender will only lend based on the lower of the purchase price or the market value. So even though it's really worth £200,000, they'll only lend against the purchase price of £150,000. That means you can borrow £112,500, put in £37,500 of your own money, and seal the deal.

You sit back, let the property out, and wait a year or two.

Now, you can approach a new lender to *refinance*. Because it's been a while since you bought the property, the purchase price is no longer an issue. They'll lend instead based on the market value, which (as we know) is £200,000. That means they'll lend you 75% of £200,000, which is £150,000.

As a result, you can take that £150,000 and:

- Repay your original loan of £112,500

- Leave £37,500 in the bank

Hey presto – the £37,500 you originally invested is back with you, and you still have 25% equity (based on the £200,000 value). That means you're effectively leaving *none of your money* in the deal, and can use that money to buy another property!

This is simplified, of course: there are actually costs associated with the purchase (stamp duty, mortgage arrangement fees, legal fees, a survey, etc.) that mean you'd end up sinking money into this deal that you can't get back out. You'd probably have needed to buy for about 30% BMV in order to truly leave no money at all tied up in the deal. Even if you only manage to buy for 15% BMV though, you've still halved the amount of money you need to save up for your next investment.

Exactly the same principle is true when you're adding value rather than buying BMV. You can take the example above, but instead imagine that instead of buying the property for £50,000 less than it's worth, you're *adding* £50,000 of value by refurbishing, extending, or solving a legal problem. In this scenario, the only difference is that there will be costs associated with adding value – so if it costs you £10,000 to refurbish and it adds £50,000 of value, you've only created an equity cushion of £40,000.

And, as I've said, you can combine the two: negotiate a discount from the market value because the property is a bit of a wreck, then add further value by refurbishing or extending.

That's the principle… and as you can see, it's a powerful one. Negotiating a discount or adding value isn't necessarily easy, but your skill in doing so can vastly reduce the amount of cash you need to find to put into the next deal.

When it comes to putting this principle into practice, there are two things you need to be aware of: timing, and the impact on your mortgage payments.

Timing your refinancing

Once you've created your equity (by buying BMV or adding value), there's always going to be a wait before you can refinance to turn that equity into cash.

If you're purely buying BMV (and not adding any extra value), that wait will be around two years. Any less time than that and your bargain purchase will be too recent: the lender's valuer will question how the property has increased in value so much in such a short space of time, and will be sceptical that it's due to your superhuman powers of negotiation.

If you're adding value too, it's possible to refinance in a shorter period of time: the works you've done give a *reason* why the value has increased, so there's no need for the lender to be dubious.

If you do want to refinance in less than a year or two, there are a couple of things you need to keep in mind.

Firstly, the absolute minimum period of time you'll have to wait is likely to be six months. There are exceptions, but lenders tend to want you to have owned the property for six months before starting your refinance application.

The other thing to consider is how you fund the *initial* purchase. Lenders don't like it if you take out a mortgage then try to refinance away in a matter of months: even if there's no early redemption penalty, they still view it as misusing what's intended to be a long-term product. You might get away with it once (or more), but you run the risk of being blacklisted once they spot a pattern (and lenders do share information between them).

That leaves you with two other options. The first is to buy in cash, which is fine if you're in a position to do so. The second is to use *bridging finance*, which is intended specifically for loans over a short period of time.

Bridging finance is more expensive than a normal mortgage: the interest rate is in the range of 0.75%–1.5% per month, and there are some chunky fees to contend with too. That leaves you with a choice: use a normal mortgage and wait a couple of years, or accept the higher bridging fees and be able to refinance and invest again in the range of 6–12 months. There's no "right" answer: you just need to run the numbers, and think about your goals to determine which is best for you.

Watch those repayments

When you're refinancing at a higher value, you're borrowing more money – which means your interest payments will increase.

In our example from earlier in this section, you were increasing borrowing from £112,500 to £150,000. Even though you still end up with 25% of the equity, your borrowing has increased by £37,500. If you're paying 5% interest on your mortgage, that takes your monthly interest payments from £468.75 to £625.

Clearly, this means that the rent needs to be high enough to support these extra repayments. If the rent is only £600, you're stuck: even if the equity is there, you can't refinance because you'd end up making a loss. (And even if you were happy making a loss for some reason, you'd fail the lender's rental cover test.)

This is an important point. Building in an equity cushion is always a good thing, even if you don't refinance (because the equity will be released when you sell, giving you a profit). But if the rent isn't high enough to support refinancing, you won't be able to speed up your portfolio growth.

Chapter 9
Buying to let

Buy a property, rent it out, profit: how am I going to drag this out to fill a whole chapter?

Actually, although buy-to-let is the safest and most straightforward property investment strategy, there's still a vast amount to think about…

Standard, single-family buy-to-let

Standard buy-to-let (BTL) is the Ant & Dec of property investment: it's been around as long as anyone can remember, has its annoying aspects, but generally can be relied on to do a solid job.

The one thing that can kill a BTL investment is voids. "Voids": your property sitting empty because no one wants to live there while you're still sending money to your mortgage lender every month. Voids are a very bad thing.

How do you avoid voids? Know your market. Buy in an area with strong, consistent rental demand, and market towards the people who want to live there. For example, you might be able to get a blinding deal on a three-bedroom house, but if it's in a dodgy part of town where no families want to live? Forget it. If you were happy to rent it to people receiving benefits it could be great, but if that isn't part of your strategy then steer clear.

If there's anything else that can mortally wound a BTL investment, it's a bad tenant. The worst kind of tenant is one who doesn't pay their rent – and it'll be weeks or months before you're allowed to start legal proceedings. End-to-end, the eviction process takes months – and in the meantime you're still paying your lender and other expenses.

If you've only got one property, you're particularly exposed to the risk of a bad tenant because they represent 100% of your property income. It's possible to buy Rent Guarantee Insurance – a policy that pays out if the tenant falls into arrears, and often also covers the legal costs of evicting them – but don't let that lull you into a false sense of security. Irrespective of whether you have insurance, you should ameliorate the risk by being very selective, reference checking the holy heck out of them, and going with your gut.

Flats vs houses

I said it earlier but it bears repeating here because I get asked all the time: I don't have any strong views about whether it's best to buy flats or houses.

Some people get very het up about it, and rant about the dangers of flats because of the lack of control you have over the service charge. Others are anti-houses because of the perceived maintenance they require.

For me, the pros and cons pretty much cancel each other out – so I'm happy to buy either, depending on which has the strongest demand in any given area. If you feel strongly one way or the other, that's fine too.

The important thing is to look at the numbers. A two-bedroom flat is often cheaper than a two-bedroom house, but that doesn't necessarily mean your return will be higher: there's a service charge to factor in, and the rent could be lower. You also need to estimate repairs for both, and consider that repairs are likely to cost you more with a house because there's more that can go wrong.

Renting to tenants in receipt of housing benefit

When someone qualifies for help from the government, they'll be eligible to receive Universal Credit (UC) – which is a roll-up of six individual benefits they might be entitled to, including Housing Benefit (HB). The rate of Housing Benefit is calculated using rates determined by Local Housing Allowance (LHA), yet many people (including the recipients) still refer to housing benefit as DSS (an outdated reference to the government department that used to issue benefits).

Yep, it's a regular acronym soup in benefit land.

It goes like this. The UK is carved up into Broad Market Rental Areas (BMRA – yup, another acronym for your collection). Within each area, an individual or family will be paid a fixed amount of LHA depending on how many bedrooms their circumstances entitle them to. For example, at the moment the government will pay £110 per week for a family to live in a three-bedroom property in Rotherham.

This will form the housing element of the family's Universal Credit entitlement, to which other benefits may be added – up to a certain cap, but let's not get into all that.

The opportunity for investors lies in the fact that the number of bedrooms is all that matters, rather than other factors that normally make a house more or less desirable.

This means that a family would receive the same amount of LHA if they lived in a three-bedroom flat in Rotherham as they would if they lived in a detached three-bedroom house in Rotherham with an acre of land, stables and a private golf course. If such a thing existed.

What's the implication for you as an investor? Well, you can pick up a three-bedroom house in Rotherham dirt cheap, price it at the exact level of LHA (because you know the government will pay it), and be guaranteed a deluge of applications because there's a huge demand for rental property in most areas of the UK and many landlords won't touch UC claimants.

(I picked this example totally out of the air, but a quick Rightmove search reveals that you can buy a perfectly serviceable three-bed terrace in Rotherham for £60,000, which would give you a gross yield of 9.5% based on a weekly rent of £110.)

But hang on a sec! If the returns are so good, why won't most landlords touch it?

Well. These days, UC is paid directly to the tenant, who's then meant to pass the rent on to the landlord (although there are sometimes ways around this). Occasionally, tenants find they have other priorities to spend the money on. Also, they often don't have the money for the rental deposit, they can cause more wear and tear than other groups, and they can disappear overnight without any warning.

None of this is meant to be discriminatory – and there are many, many landlords with big portfolios of UC tenants who do very nicely indeed. But it's a fact that the risks, plus the effort involved in helping tenants navigate the hellish bureaucracy around the whole thing, can put landlords off. The plus side? It leaves the rewards on the table for those who want to make it part of their business model.

Student lets

Ah, students. Dossers who spend all day sitting around stubbing out fags on the wallpaper while they save their energy for an out-of-control house party at night.

Or... not? With average student debt approaching the average weekly wage of a mediocre footballer (hmm, there must be a better comparison than that), students are getting a lot more serious than in the days when they were paid to be there.

They're more demanding too. When I was a student, we had single beds and furnishings older than we were. These days, students won't settle for anything less than double beds, a flat-screen TV in every bedroom, and fixtures 'n' fittings straight out of a House of Fraser catalogue.

This means you can no longer shove a bunch of students in a grotty old house and relieve them of their student loan for the privilege, but there can still be a lot of money to be made. That's because you're charging by the room, and the level of rent is generally within some tight norms in any given student town – and can bear no resemblance to what you'd get for letting to a family.

Let's go to Liverpool for this example. The three-bedroom LHA rate for a property in central Liverpool is £120.82 per week. But if you had a three-bedroom mid-terrace property with two reception rooms, you could convert one into an extra bedroom and have four students each paying you £80 per week. That's a full £200 more than the LHA rate, every week.

The other major benefit of students is the predictability with which they come and go. You'll know exactly what week they'll move out at the end of their academic year, by which point you'll already have the next year's tenants signed up. Beat that.

The downsides? There's no killer downside, but lots of niggles. For a start, the £80 per week includes bills – so that's an extra cost to consider. Unrelated people sharing a house means the property is classed as a House in Multiple Occupation (HMO – we'll discuss this next), which can require a compulsory licence and, in some areas, need planning permission if you're changing it from a single family let. Students do cause more wear and tear than families, and properties definitely need to be furnished – which costs money upfront and increases your maintenance budget too.

Getting finance to buy a house for students can be tricky, as some lenders restrict the number of bedrooms or shy away from HMOs completely. Then there's the demand side: with a lot of purpose-built student accommodation now being built, will there be less demand for traditional student housing? And if you can't find tenants for your student house, is it in an area where you'd be able to find a family to rent it? Would the lower rent paid by a family still make you a profit?

So students can be highly profitable, but if you get your investment wrong it can cause you a headache worse than a Freshers' Week hangover.

HMOs

An HMO is when more than one "household" shares a kitchen or bathroom – with the most common examples being a student house, a group of friends sharing a house, or a house that's being let by the room. There are actually different definitions of what constitutes an HMO for different purposes, but this basic definition will work for us.

HMOs come with their fair share of extra regulations. If the property has five or more people living there, you'll need a license – and some councils require licenses even for smaller HMOs. In some areas, HMOs are so prevalent that councils are refusing permission for single family houses to be converted into new HMOs completely.

Why the regulations? Well, HMOs are more of a safety risk than single lets, and licences ensure that fire escape routes are in place, gas and electrical appliances are safe, and the house is being run professionally.

As we saw with student houses, HMOs can be highly profitable. By packing in as many bedrooms as possible, the total rent you can get from an HMO can dwarf what you'd get from the same house as a single let.

This profit is the landlord's reward for doing what can be a very effort-intensive job. Apart from the regulatory burden of making sure the HMO meets council standards, wear-and-tear will be higher than if the property was let to a family, rent needs to be collected from each tenant individually, and bills are often included in the rent so the landlord needs to keep on top of this paperwork too.

There's also the issue of tenant turnover. Depending on the type of tenant you target, they can often be quite transient – and every time someone leaves there are marketing expenses, costs to reference check the new tenant, and the possibility of a void period. Combine this with increased maintenance costs, and the profits aren't as high as they might first seem.

An HMO can still generate a lot of cash if costs are realistically estimated and voids are minimised. The secret of a successful HMO? As with other investments, know your market. If you want to cut down on hassle and target young professionals, buy in a desirable area and furnish the property to the standard they'll expect. If you want to target the LHA market, buy cheap, go for hardwearing furnishings, and have systems in place to collect rent efficiently and stay on top of any issues.

Holiday lets

Moving on, let's recover from all this HMO chat by going to the seaside. Or the Lake District, or a nice cottage in the countryside. Because the British holiday is alive and well, especially in more austere times (and when Ryanair has put many people off flying for life). Holiday lets are becoming increasingly popular as an investment, and may find further favour over the next few years as they're exempt from the restrictions on finance relief.

Successful holiday lets are about three things: location, marketing and pricing. If you buy in a popular location, you should fill up the prime weeks of the year relatively easily. But the returns come from successfully filling the "shoulder months" – times when you have a realistic chance of some demand, but it's not peak season. That's where marketing comes in.

Pricing is vital because you'll want to vary your rates throughout the year to maximise occupancy. Luckily, your competitors will by necessity be very open about their own pricing, so you'll know how to position your property competitively.

The obvious downside of holiday lets is that you'll never know exactly what your rental income will be, because your occupancy rate will be unknown. There might also be relatively high costs to factor in – you'll need to pay for cleaning between tenants, and maybe a managing agent to deal with check-ins if you don't live locally. Then there are your marketing expenses, and the consideration that your mortgage (if you use one) may be more expensive because there are fewer lenders in the holiday let market.

The flipside is that you'll be spreading your risk – one bad tenant can't mess you up for months on end. And if you've worked out your numbers based on a conservative occupancy rate, you can keep tweaking your pricing and marketing to boost your occupancy and therefore your profit.

As you might have gathered from all this talk about tweaking prices, marketing for the quieter months, dealing with constant check-ins and check-outs and so on, a holiday let needs to be run like a business. Using a managing agent can help, but even if they're competent they're not going to work as hard to maximise occupancy as you would. After all, an empty week might mean £500 to you but it's only £50 to them.

Then again, if it's sitting empty you can always take a nice break there yourself.

Chapter 10
Buying to sell

Buying to sell (or "flipping") isn't, in my opinion, technically property *investing*. Investing implies putting money into something for a reasonable period of time in anticipation of a return, whereas buying-to-sell is *trading:* buying something purely because you think you can very quickly sell it for more. For someone who buys to sell, property is effectively held as "stock" rather than an asset.

Trading is more of a "job" – even if an enjoyable and well-paid one – because (unlike investing) if you stop actively doing deals you completely stop earning. That's why the focus of this book has been buy-to-let, but having an understanding of buying to sell is still a valuable tool in a property investor's arsenal.

Why buy to sell?

The benefit of buying to sell is that (if you get it right) it means immediate cash in the bank. If you're desperate to quit your job right now, it's the only strategy that would allow you to do so: two deals per year earning a net profit of £20,000 each could replace your wage, whereas two properties making a monthly profit of £300 won't do much for you in the short term.

While quitting your job and doing those deals right now is technically possible, I'd still file it under "seriously bad idea". Too many episodes of Homes Under The Hammer can make you think that everything will work out perfectly and be wrapped up nicely within half an hour, but in reality just one bad project can ruin you if it's your only source of income. Plenty of people are full-time property traders and do very nicely, but you want to be able to learn the business and make mistakes without it affecting your livelihood.

Alongside a job though, buying to sell can be a great way of generating extra lumps of cash. Indeed, some people run a parallel strategy: do a couple of buy-to-sell projects per year, invest the profits into buy-to-let, and put the original capital back into the next trade.

Even if trading isn't really your thing at all, it's worth having an understanding of how it works — just in case a dream opportunity falls into your lap while you're looking for buy-to-let investments.

Finding opportunities

Finding a buy-to-sell opportunity is largely a case of finding a property in the "investor" market (where a hard bargain can be driven) and improving it so it appeals to the "owner-occupier" market (where emotion rules the day). Historically the place to do this has been auctions, but auctions are now such popular hunting grounds for anyone looking for "a project" that prices are often bid up to a level where there's no profit potential left.

As a result, you can't ignore other methods of finding opportunities – such as through estate agents, or (if you're willing to put in the work) direct marketing methods like leaflets through doors and adverts in the local paper.

If you do decide to stick to buying at auction, you need to be prepared for the ways in which it differs from a normal property purchase.

Auction newbies are often worried about scratching their nose and ending up the proud owner of a house-boat in the Highlands, and it's kind of a valid concern: you're legally committed to the sale as soon as the hammer falls. You have to pay 10% and exchange contracts on the same day, and you'll be in all sorts of trouble if you need to get out of it later.

For that reason, you've got to do all your research in advance. Auction houses will release the legal pack ahead of the auction date, giving you the chance to look through for showstopping problems and get your solicitor to take a look if you need to. There'll also be days when the property is available for viewings. Auctions operate on the principle of "buyer beware", so if you buy somewhere with a tangled web of legal problems or only three walls because you failed to do your research, you're not going to get anywhere by moaning about it later.

Always remember: if a property is at auction, it's there because there's a problem with it. If you haven't spot-ted the problem, it's not because it's some kind of amazing gem of a deal – it's because you just haven't looked hard enough.

It's your job to do your homework and work out in advance what the problem is, if you can be bothered to fix it, and how much you should bid once you've taken into account the cost of putting things right.

Other than that, success at auction simply involves remembering two golden rules:

- Know your price, and don't bid above it. Just because others are willing to pay more, it doesn't mean they're right and you're wrong: they might have different buying criteria, might be a novice with no buying criteria at all, or even be buying it to live in (in which case their priorities will be totally different).

- Sit on your hands when you're not bidding. Just in case.

Financing

A mortgage isn't an appropriate way of funding a buy-to-sell project. They're intended to be held for multiple years, but you only really want to own the property for a few months while you get it ready to sell again – so while you *could* arrange a mortgage under false pretences, you run the risk of getting blacklisted when they realise what you're up to.

In any case, properties that need work doing often aren't mortgageable — because you can only get a mortgage on a property that's habitable. And if you're buying at auction, the 28 days you have to come up with the money won't be long enough to arrange a mortgage even if you wanted to.

As a result, there are two main ways to finance buy-to-sell projects: cash, or bridging finance.

Cash is straightforward, of course. Bridging finance we came across earlier: it's a form of short-term lending with rates in the range of 0.75%–1.5% per month, plus fees. It's expensive when compared to a mortgage, but it's just a cost that needs to be factored in: is it *really* expensive if it allows you to do a deal where you walk away with thousands of pounds in profit, even after paying the bridging costs?

Making a profit

Running a buy-to-sell project, even if you're not doing the actual hands-on work yourself, is hard graft. So if you're going to put all that effort in, you'd better make sure you're going to be rewarded with a healthy profit.

The key to making a profit is to start with the price you can sell it for when the work is done, and work back from there.

Start by calculating your realistic selling price (which can be done in the same way that you'd assess the market value of any property). Then you can deduct all your costs: the cost of doing the refurbishment, any finance costs, stamp duty, legal fees, agents' fees when you sell, and everything else you can think of.

The number that's left has to account for both the price of buying the property *and* the profit you've got left at the end. So if you start with a selling price of £300,000 and come up with £120,000 in costs, that leaves you with £180,000. If you buy the property for £180,000, you're left with nothing – so you have to decide the price you're willing to pay *below* that number that will leave you with a profit you're happy with.

Then it's just a case of keeping the project on time and on budget. I say "just", but of course that's no mean feat. Your first project is unlikely to make a lot of money because you'll make a fair few mistakes in managing it – but you'll learn from them, and your operation will become more slick (and more profitable) every time.

Selling

Once the property is gleaming and looking like something out of Grand Designs, the hard work is done – but you don't make a profit until you actually sell it.

It's critical to keep this fact in mind the whole way through the project, and use it to guide the decisions you make. When you come to sell, you want it to appeal to the largest possible number of people – which means making layout and design decisions that are likely to suit the majority of your target market. It's also something to keep in mind when you're buying in the first place: if your costs accumulate to the point where you need to sell for £20,000 more than comparable properties in order to make a profit, it could end up sitting on the market for a long time. And while it sits, you've got cash tied up and/or bridging fees ticking upwards by the day.

At the point of selling, it's well worth spending a bit of money and effort in presenting it as well as you possibly can: *you* might be a totally rational investor, but you need an owner-occupier to fall in love with it. Ideally, you need two owner-occupiers to fall in love with it and bid each other up to a level that makes you an even bigger profit.

Professional photos are the easiest win here: for a cost of about £100, you can get photos that put almost everything else on Rightmove to shame – which will translate to more viewings, and eventually more offers. Ideally, "staging" the property with furniture (bought or rented) will make an even bigger difference.

Once the winning offer has been accepted, it's not quite "done deal" yet: remember, about a third of transactions fall through before completing. If you can sell to a cash buyer or someone who isn't in a chain, that will remove a portion of the risk. Whoever you're selling to, don't be afraid to keep pushing your solicitor and the estate agent: these things have a tendency to grind to a halt if you're not always on people's backs, so a bit of pressure can end up putting the money in your bank account weeks earlier than would have otherwise happened.

PART 3:
MINDSET

Chapter 11
Education

Education should always be a priority – whether you're just getting started and have everything to learn, or picking up titbits to add to your existing body (or head, rather) of knowledge.

But how should you educate yourself in property? Pay for it? Learn it on the job? Or teach yourself from free resources online?

The scary thing is how many people choose "none of the above". Legally, letting a property is a big deal: by creating a tenancy, you're giving the occupant rights that supersede your own. Yet people gaily charge in without doing even a soupçon of Googling first.

If in-person learning is more your style, there are courses run by the likes of the National Residential Landlords Association, which cover those legal and procedural basics. The problem is that no one will ever go out of their way to entice you to go on one.

That's not the case for courses that promise to tell you how to make millions in property with little effort and none of your own money. Those types of emails pile up in my inbox, although I'm pretty sure I never signed up to find out about one.

Courses are a contentious subject in property, because everyone and his brother seems to run one. Some of them are entirely legit, but if you dig into the claims of some of the so-called "gurus", you'll often find they barely own any property themselves. And anyway, if they were making soooo many millions from property, why would they be trying to lure you to a draughty seminar room off the M4?

Courses aren't a replacement for reading books and browsing forums online (that should be the bare min-imum an active investor does, and I link to some good resources at the end), but a good course can be a worthwhile investment. As long as it doesn't lure you in with false promises, it can give you valuable new ideas and save tens of hours trying to piece fragments together online – and sometimes an investment in yourself is the best investment you can make.

Other than saving time, one of the main benefits I think people get out of courses is accountability. For a start, if you've dropped £1,000 on a course, you have an incentive to follow through and make sure you haven't wasted your money. But you'll also meet people on the course who can hold you accountable – and the best coaches will check in afterwards to see how you're getting on.

So there's nothing wrong with paying for education, as long as you do some research into the track record of the teacher first. But you'll also find that an unusually large number of people in property are willing to help you for free. I have no idea why – perhaps it's because it's not a zero sum game. If you're in Brighton, there's no harm in someone from Chester sharing their strategy with you (although, of course, it might not work in your area).

However you do it, make sure you keep educating yourself – and sharing your own knowledge with others.

Chapter 12
Networking

Ah, networking: a way to keep tatty hotels and name-tag manufacturers in business. But also, if you approach it the right way, a way to supercharge your property business. Because while property is about bricks and numbers, above all it's about people.

A lot of people approach it completely the wrong way around though – and as a result they create a bad experience for other people and don't get much out of it themselves.

Even though I'm hardly Captain Sociable, I can't deny the huge value in networking the *right* way.

Here are a few ways to do just that…

Offer value before you ask for value

Networking has negative connotations for many people: they equate it with a room full of people greedily trying to find others they can use to further their own self-interest.

And you know what? In any room there will be people doing exactly that. Chances are you've experienced someone cornering you and telling you exactly what they're working on without asking a single thing about you. Or maybe someone has tried to find out straight away if you can help them, then disappeared as soon as they decide you can't. Neither is a pleasant position to be in.

Faced with this, it's tempting to conclude that you need to become one of these mercenary, self-interested people too – because networking's all about self-promotion and furthering your own business, right?

WRONG! You don't need to become one of those people. There's another way.

Instead of looking for help, approach every interaction thinking about how you can help the other person. All relationships are based on an exchange of value – whether that value is support, friendship, respect, money or knowledge – and you should give value before asking for it in return.

Even if the only value you can offer is being interested in the other person and making them feel good about themselves, do that rather than droning on about yourself and how great you are/how awful your problems are. At worst, you've just made the world a slightly better place; at best, you've made a new contact who you might be able to ask for help in future.

Build it before you need it

Need to meet a joint venture partner? A mortgage expert? Someone to guide you through buying at auction?

Bad news: if you need help now, you're already too late. It takes time to build a network, and if you launch into it to meet a need you've got right now, you're going to be disappointed. Sure, you might get lucky – people in property are extremely helpful – but if you disappear again until next time you need something, you'll have to start all over again.

In short, do you think networking is unnecessary for you right now? Then it's exactly the time you should start doing it.

Follow up

The day after an event, follow up with everyone you spoke to. A short email like this is all you need:

"Hi Mary, it was a pleasure to meet you last night. We spoke about the new block of flats you're developing in Rugby, and it was really interesting to hear how it's coming along. A friend of mine is a letting agent nearby, so let me know if it'd be helpful for me to put you in touch. Hope to catch up again soon, Rob."

A reminder of your conversation, an offer of help (if appropriate), and an invitation to stay in contact. That's all you need. If it feels weird to send an email (or you didn't get their contact details), you could always send a LinkedIn request with that kind of message as part of your invitation. It beats the hell out of "I'd like to add you to my professional network", and isn't much more effort really.

Try to follow up occasionally with everyone you meet. Even if it's hard to see how you'll benefit each other in the near future, you never know where people will end up. Some people you'll want to become close to, and others you'll just send a quick "hi" or a link to an article they might like every couple of months.

Get online

Networking in person is great, but it doesn't scale: there are only so many events you can go to before your spouse leaves you or you totally lose track of who's been fired in The Apprentice.

Connections you make online aren't as deep as with people you meet in person, but the benefit is greater reach. If you were crazy you could go to five events a week and talk to 50 people each time, for a total reach of 250 people. Online you can reach thousands, constantly.

Both online and offline networking are therefore valuable in different ways. That's why I co-founded an online community called Property Hub (**property-hub.net/forum**).

When networking in online communities, don't worry about asking silly questions. Do a search first to make sure your question hasn't been answered already, and if it hasn't then don't hold back: however basic it may be, there'll be others who can learn from the answers too. Even if you're too shy to post anything at all, you'll be amazed by the amount of knowledge you pick up from just browsing a few topics every day.

Another form of online networking is just emailing people out of the blue. It might feel like an intrusion, but there's nothing wrong with cold-emailing someone who's written a forum post you enjoyed, or has a blog you follow, or who you just happen to know operates in an area you'll be passing through. Granted, it's much easier if you already have some visibility online from actively contributing to a community – but if you send a nice friendly email, there's no reason it can't work anyway.

Then there are platforms like Twitter and Facebook, which I'm not active on but are heavily used by many investors. The point is, though, that once you start looking there are people talking about property on just about every platform you can think of. It's just a case of finding the one that's the most natural fit for you: if it feels like a chore then you won't do it, and the key to successful online networking is to do it (even if just for five minutes) every day.

Chapter 13
Playing to your strengths

What makes property a pretty unique industry is the number of ways you can make money from it.

This book is about investment, for example. But aside from investing, here's a non-exhaustive list of other ways you can get involved with property:

- Estate agent

- Conveyancer

- Interior designer

- Mortgage broker

- Deal sourcer

- Architect

- Surveyor

- Insurance expert

- Builder

- Inventory clerk

Even within the realm of investment, there are myriad ways to make money.

For example, buying to sell is very different from buying to let – in terms of the skills you need, the type of risk you take on, and the way in which you make your money. Even within basic buy-to-let, renting to housing benefit tenants will be an entirely different experience from renting to young professionals – the issues you face will be different, and the risk profile is very different.

We talked about goals earlier on, but it's worth going beyond goals and thinking about your abilities and personality too. You might decide that direct marketing, for example, is the perfect way to reach your goals. But are you the kind of person who'll be comfortable negotiating face-to-face with vendors in financial difficulty who are eying you with suspicion? If not, it's probably not a good idea – even if it's the perfect way to reach your goals if you look purely at the numbers.

Your attitude to risk is another area worth thinking about more. Or more accurately, your tolerance for different types of risk. All investments are risky (no risk, no return), but the types of risk can be very different.

Buying at auction, for example, is seen by some people as nail-bitingly risky because you're (by definition) paying more than anyone else is willing to pay, and you're expected to complete immediately. But if you spoke to an experienced auction buyer, they'd tell you that they've already done their research, they know what works, and if it all goes wrong they can just stick it back into auction and get most of their money back.

That person might see a nice, bog standard family let in a nice suburban area as far more risky: what if a big local employer closes, or the family stops paying rent and you've got a six-month wait to evict them?

Then even within single family buy-to-lets, is letting to people on housing benefit more or less risky than letting to a working family? With people on benefits there's often a perception of antisocial behaviour and doing a runner without paying the rent, but on the other hand you know there's a near limitless supply of tenants – couldn't that be seen as better than having a lovely house that'd suit a nice working family, when there are no nice working families to be found?

None of these things is really riskier than another – but they're different types of risk. Before jumping into a particular type of investment because it seems like a good idea on paper, think about what's most likely to keep you awake at night. If you won't be able to sleep for worrying about people on benefits starting a marijuana farm in your living room – even if that's totally irrational – that type of investing might not be right for you, however attractive the yields.

If you're lacking skills in a particular area, you can always consider a joint venture with someone who has a complementary skill set. Often this happens natur-ally within families – you often see father-and-daugh-ter teams where one has a head for figures and the other has the hands-on skills. If you don't already know suitable joint venture partners, that's where networking can really pay off.

Remember: you can't be good at everything. And while it isn't a good idea to have gaping holes in your knowledge and skills, it makes sense to focus on what you're best at.

So think about how you can work with others to play to your strengths. You can find the deals, he can do the building work. She can crunch the numbers, you can manage the tenants. There's really no limit to the teams you can put together.

As you continue your reading and research into property, think beyond what's worked for other people and consider what makes the most sense for you.

Chapter 14
Systems

Things rarely go as planned, especially in property. If you're not careful, it's easy to get sucked into the endless details and day-to-day dilemmas, and lose sight of the big picture. When you should be thinking about what to buy next or what big demographic trends you should be planning for, you're probably answering a call about a blocked sink or filling in some nonsense form for the council.

What separates the good from the great is the ability to rise above the day-to-day jobs and focus on the unique value that only YOU can provide.

At heart, this means delegating. But delegation can be disastrous if the person who's doing the job keeps calling to check things with you, or lets things slip. Managing your staff and correcting their mistakes can be more time-consuming than doing it yourself in the first place.

In fact, it's probably a short, catastrophic experiment with outsourcing that causes many people to be stuck working IN their business instead of ON their business. And as Michael Gerber says in the classic business book The E-Myth Revisited, if you do everything in the business and can't be removed from it, you haven't really created a business: you've just created a job for yourself.

To avoid falling into this trap, imagine you're setting up a prototype franchise: your job is to reduce the entire business to a set of written systems that can be executed by average people.

Conversely though, you shouldn't try to outsource too early. Gerber recommends you do every job yourself, write a clear set of instructions for it, and then hire someone to take it over. If they can't get the hang of what they're meant to be doing, it's probably not their fault – it's the fault of the system. Keep on revising and simplifying until everything runs smoothly.

It might seem that a business run from an operations manual will lack heart. But because you did every job yourself first, your own style and personality will be stamped all over it. And the systems don't have to be totally rigid: one of the rules could be "If X happens, use your initiative to make the tenant happy as long as it doesn't cost more than £100."

Once you start thinking in terms of systems, you'll find countless ways to stop doing dreary tasks and spend your time focusing on what matters – even if you own just a few properties. Instead of waiting in for tradesmen, install key safes outside your properties. Use a call-answering service as a "tenant hotline" so you don't get bothered on your mobile all day. Write down the exact process you use to advertise for new tenants so you don't forget it for the months when you're not using it – and then just pass the document to someone else to execute if you're busy when the situation next arises.

For some reason I haven't worked out yet, people in property often have serious perfectionist tendencies – which makes it difficult to let go. What if an employee sends an email with a typo in it? Or they end up booking a tradesman who costs £20 more than you would have found by shopping around?

Obviously, neither of those things really matter – if someone else can do a job 80% as well as you can, let them get on with it and focus on the things that make a big difference. But as Tony Hseih, the CEO of Zappos.com says, don't outsource your core competency. In other words, if analysing potential deals is what you do brilliantly and it makes all the difference to your business, keep doing it. If not, outsource it.

So as you build your business (and it *is* a business – just one buy-to-let property is a mini-business of its own), think about what you could systemise so you can start working ON your business instead of IN it.

Chapter 15
People

As I may have mentioned a few times already, property is a bricks business and a numbers business, but overall it's a people business. You'll buy from people, rent and sell to people, and have all kinds of people working for you in the process.

That's not to say you have to be a gregarious, extroverted type to succeed in property. As we've already talked about, the beauty of property is that you can find your own niche based on your particular skills and personality type.

You will, though, need to have a basic understanding of what makes people tick. And that's where it's immensely helpful to understand what motivates people.

People are motivated by money, of course. But that doesn't mean you can pay your solicitor a lot of money, treat them badly, and expect them to do a stellar job for you. People are also motivated by feeling appreciated, having the opportunity to do their best work, and feeling part of a bigger mission.

You don't need me to tell you to be nice to people, I'm sure. Yet there's a perception in property that you've got to be tough, and loud, and brutal to succeed – that if you show weakness, it'll be exploited.

There *are* people like that, and sometimes they do succeed. In my experience though, most successful people I've met in property are kind and helpful and polite to everyone they deal with. And when the chips are down, the "nice guys" are far more likely to get people bending over backwards to make things work out for them.

Your property team

Here's a non-exhaustive list of the people you'll be working with in a typical transaction:

An estate agent. If you're buying a property that's listed for sale rather than seeking out off-market opportunities, dealing with estate agents goes with the territory. Although they're working for the vendor rather than for you, their main motivation is to get the property sold so they can get their commission. If you can make their life easier by being professional, friendly, and doing what you say you'll do, they've got an incentive to call you rather than anyone else when the next deal comes along.

A vendor. Messages filtered through agents and solicitors can quickly become a game of Chinese whispers, so it's often handy to have a direct line of communication with the vendor – even if you're going through an agent. It's not always possible, but sometimes they'll be very happy to swap numbers so you can nip problems in the bud and keep things moving quickly.

A mortgage broker. A good broker will advise you on the pros and cons of every financing option, and possibly come up with creative solutions you'd never have considered. Some brokers are tied to a particular lender, or make their money solely through the commissions that lenders pay. My preference is to work with a broker who charges you a fee: that way, even if they get a kickback from the lender too, that won't be as much of a factor in their decision about which lender to recommend. That's purely a matter of opinion, though.

A solicitor. Solicitors (or specialist conveyancers) are massively important in any transaction, and it's vital to maintain a good relationship with a solicitor who suits your style of working. You want a solicitor who's on top of all the details and won't let anything slide, but at the same time isn't overly pernickety or combative – it's easy to spend weeks where nothing happens while both sides' solicitors send passive-aggressive emails to each other. Stay on side with your solicitor by being responsive, giving them what they need, and remembering that they're a human – not just a paper-pushing machine.

A surveyor. Surveyors can be frustrating because they tend to provide you with the world's most cautious and equivocal information so that they can't be sued if they miss something. Even on a new-build house, they'll tend to produce reams of possible defects – and it's hard to tell what's a dealbreaker and what isn't. Being chummy with your surveyor should make it easier to get "off the record" advice that makes a lot more sense than their official report.

A builder. A good builder is one of the most valuable assets you can have, so if you find one, keep hold of them. Be fair, be reasonable, pay quickly, and don't give the impression you suspect they're ripping you off at every turn (while making sure they *don't* rip you off at every turn).

An accountant. The more closely you can work with your accountant, the more they'll understand your goals and the better advice they'll be able to give you. If you get seriously into property, a specialist property accountant is a great member of your team: they'll know every last allowance that can be claimed, and exactly what will and won't be viewed with suspicion.

Tenants are people too

This isn't a book about being a landlord, but landlord-ism comes as part of the job – albeit a part of the job that you can outsource if you want to. Your tenants pay the rent, which pays your mortgage, which buys you an asset... so it's in your interest to treat them well.

There are two schools of thought when it comes to interacting with tenants. One says that if you get to know them as people, they're less likely to try any funny business – they'll see you as a human being, not a faceless money-gouging machine.

The other says that it's best to keep things strictly professional – or to put a letting agent between the two of you so you don't have any interaction at all.

When I was starting out I used to self-manage, but I'm now at the point where I use a letting agent for everything and have never had any kind of interaction with my current tenants. Neither is "better" (it's a case of whatever works best for you at the time), but I don't feel like I've lost anything from not having a personal relationship. And indeed, when I was a tenant, I couldn't have cared less whether or not my landlord was a nice chap: I just wanted things to be fixed when they broke.

Whether you're buddy-buddy or hands-off, you need to make sure your tenants are treated well. If you use a letting agent, that means making sure they're being responsive to anything that needs to be done. Without tenants, you don't have any income – so react quickly to any maintenance, be fair, and never lose sight of the fact that they can take their business elsewhere if they're not happy.

PULLING THE TRIGGER

There's a saying that goes, "Fools rush in where angels fear to tread."

There's another saying about "paralysis by analysis".

You want to be somewhere between the two.

Because let's not beat about the bush here – whacking down a chunk of your savings and taking on an even bigger chunk of debt is a bloody scary thing. You shouldn't take it lightly. At the same time, though, you have to pull the trigger one day – otherwise you'll still be daydreaming about the riches you could get from property when you're 70. (And it's not as easy to get a mortgage when you're 70.)

Near the start of this book, I delivered a rambling monologue about Property Ladder. Now, those people were fools: they got swept up in the hysteria of the markets, rushed down to an auction house and bid like crazy – and probably didn't even fill the back of a moderately sized envelope with their calculations.

By reading this book, you've demonstrated that you're not that kind of person. In a minute I'm going to direct you towards all kinds of further reading and resources, where you can read for hours on end about different strategies. And you should. But at some point, you've got to put the books down, go out and buy a property.

Your first deal probably won't be the absolute deal of the century. It doesn't matter. As long as it works for you (by making you money rather than costing each month), you'll be inspired to go on and do a little bit better with the next one, and you'll have learnt heaps from the process.

What if it's a complete turkey? Well, you can mitigate against that happening in the first place:

- If you've been networking, you might be able to run your potential purchase past a friendly expert.

- If in doubt, get a survey: it'll cost you a few hundred quid, but you'll know there's not some horrendous flaw you've missed.

- Put a fake advert on Gumtree to assess rental demand.

- Use the calculations from earlier in this book to work out how much you should be paying. If you know the rent you can achieve and what your target yield is, you'll arrive at a purchase price you know you can't go above.

And even if everything goes wrong – the boiler blows up in the first month, your tenants stop paying rent – and you lose money during the first year, you'll have gained heaps of experience, and you'll still have plenty more years to make money from your property.

Like a bad haircut, problems tend to grow out. If you've overpaid, house prices will go up in line with inflation in the long term. If you've over-leveraged yourself, you can pay the debt down over time – and inflation will erode it in real terms anyway. And if you've totally miscalculated your target market and struggle to attract tenants, there's a near-endless list of things you can do to appeal to different groups of people. Or just drop the rent and take the lower yield on the chin.

So, good luck! And please, please write to me (rob@propertygeek.net.) once you've bought your first property and you see the money coming in – it'll make me very happy to know you're taking action.

Now, go pull that trigger!

LEARN WHAT'S WORKING IN PROPERTY RIGHT NOW

This book is designed to give you a fun, accessible overview of property investment. There's always plenty more to learn, though – especially as the market is changing all the time.

To deepen your knowledge and keep up with all the changes, there are two things you should do.

First, sign up for my weekly newsletter at **propertygeek.net/newsletter**. Every Sunday I share the top property stories of the week with a short explanation of why they matter.

Then, visit **propertyhub.net** (which I co-founded) where we publish free courses, videos, a weekly podcast, and more – and you can join the Property Hub community to benefit from the knowledge of thousands of other investors.

I'll see you there!

FURTHER
LEARNING

I hope this book has left you with a better understanding of what property investment involves – and I hope you'll be fizzing with ideas for which route you want to go down. But this has been a high-level overview, and there's still an immense amount to learn.

Fortunately, there's a wealth of free and inexpensive information out there. So, whatever you do, don't plonk down £10,000 for some fancy training course until you're sure your answers aren't lurking somewhere in these…

BOOKS

I know this sounds awful, but there are no property books I'd unreservedly recommend other than my own – partially because so much has changed recently and I can't guarantee they're up-to-date. So, self-plugging ahoy…

The direct follow-up to this book is **The Complete Guide To Property Investment: How to survive and thrive in the new world of buy-to-let**. It's about four times the length of this book, and includes… well, as the title implies, pretty much everything. As the title also implies, it was written after the fundamental changes to the buy-to-let market were introduced in

2015 (and is updated annually). That means it's geared towards making smart, strategic investments that work today and will stand the test of time.

If you enjoyed this book, it's the natural next step. Find out more at **propertygeek.net/complete**.

If you'd like to dive into the nitty-gritty of letting and managing a property, take a look at my book **How To Be A Landlord: The definitive guide to letting and managing your rental property**. It takes you through every practical and legal step you need to complete if you're doing it yourself, and has guidance for selecting and working with a letting agent if I make it sound like too much hard work. Find out more at **propertygeek.net/landlordbook**.

My other book is **Beyond The Bricks: The inside story of how nine everyday investors found financial freedom through property**. It consists of long-form interviews with successful property investors, all of whom have taken markedly different routes to building up their life-changing portfolios. Their stories and case studies explore the human side of property investment, give you an insight into the many options out there, and demonstrate what it takes to succeed. Find out more at **propertygeek.net/beyond**.

MAGAZINES

Me again... I co-founded **The Property Hub Magazine** (propertyhub.net/magazine) and write a regular column for it. It's published every other month, and is made up of news, case studies, in-depth opinion pieces and deep-dives on mortgages, tax and lettings. For £5 per issue including delivery, you can't go far wrong.

There's also **Property Investor News** (property-investor-news.com), which is a bit more high-level and macro. It's not something I read, but it's widely recommended in the investor community.

COMMUNITIES

Property Hub (propertyhub.net) is a community I co-founded, and is the fastest growing (and friendliest) forum in the UK with over 45,000 members. There's active, well-informed debate every day, and it's a great place to both get specific questions answered and keep on top of what the most switched-on investors are thinking.

Another worthy community is **Property Tribes** (propertytribes.com), where founder Vanessa does an excellent job of sharing the latest news and talking points.

And there's **Property 118** (property118.com), where the comments section is always lively and lots of serious landlords hang out.

Finally, there's a huge array of Facebook groups. If you search groups for "property" you'll find a bunch, with the **UK BMV Group** being the biggest. There's a wealth of information being shared, but be careful: in common with Facebook in general, there are a lot of claims that you'll want to take with a pinch of salt too.

PODCASTS

Oh, these are mine again. Does it still count as self-promotion when it's nearly all free?

The Property Podcast (propertyhub.net/podcast) goes out every Thursday morning – and has done for the last eight years, so if you like it there are lots of back episodes to work through.

My co-host and I talk about a different property topic every week, and we also share useful resources and discuss the latest news. It's a focused and fun half hour, and an effort-free way to keep on top of everything that's going on. Every Tuesday, there's an extra episode where you get the chance to put a question to us on "Ask Rob & Rob".

If you're not totally sure how to listen to a podcast, don't worry – just follow the link above and you'll find instructions for how to subscribe so every episode gets automatically delivered to your phone.

Printed in Germany
by Amazon Distribution
GmbH, Leipzig

22379742R00100